HOLDING POWER

HOLDING POWER

BUILDING LONG LASTING CUSTOMER RELATIONSHIPS WITH THE PUSH OF A BUTTON

PETER J. TURPEL

Published by Advantage, Charleston, South Carolina.
Member of Advantage Media Group.

ADVANTAGE is a registered trademark and the Advantage colophon is a trademark of Advantage Media Group, Inc.

Printed in the United States of America.

ISBN: 978-1-59932-225-4
LCCN: 2011907251

This publication is designed to provide accurate and authoritative information in regard to the subject matter covered. It is sold with the understanding that the publisher is not engaged in rendering legal, accounting, or other professional services. If legal advice or other expert assistance is required, the services of a competent professional person should be sought.

 Advantage Media Group is proud to be a part of the Tree Neutral® program. Tree Neutral offsets the number of trees consumed in the production and printing of this book by taking proactive steps such as planting trees in direct proportion to the number of trees used to print books. To learn more about Tree Neutral, please visit www.treeneutral.com. To learn more about Advantage's commitment to being a responsible steward of the environment, please visit www.advantagefamily.com/green

Advantage Media Group is a leading publisher of business, motivation, and self-help authors. Do you have a manuscript or book idea that you would like to have considered for publication? Please visit www.amgbook.com or call 1.866.775.1696

*To my parents, who gave me the gift of getting along
and savoring the human experience.*

Joseph and Louise Turpel–honeymoon, 1945.

About the Author

Peter J. Turpel is founder, president and chief executive officer of Phone On-Hold® Marketing Systems, with clients nationwide, throughout Canada, and in Puerto Rico. A former radio personality, he spun the Top 40 and hosted morning and afternoon drive shows before moving into radio station management, and he has worked as a professional commercial voice-over actor. In the early 1980s, he helped to pioneer the concept of producing effective audio for business on-hold networks, professionally created and tailored to the client's needs. He is one of the originating founders and has served as chairman of the International On-Hold Messaging Association, which sets industry standards for providers worldwide: **www.ohma.org**

About the Company

Phone On-Hold® Marketing Systems, founded in 1984, offers professional audio studio production to create and make the most of on-hold communication networks for businesses. Its resources include creative consultants, professional voice-over actors, music licensing, an understanding of emerging telecommunication technology, and customer service. At this writing, we are the only company of our kind in the world to be ISO 9001:2008 certified in quality management. This is a coveted worldwide certification ensuring that business operations are in place.

Phone On-Hold® Marketing Systems, is the first on-hold provider to offer daily national, sports and entertainment news in the United States. To learn how you can make the most of your on-hold communication network, through enhancing your brand and your customers' experience with your business, call us at 1-800-465-3102. Or visit our website: **www.phoneonhold.com.**

Our Philosophy

Business has many communication channels: radio, television, print, direct mail, the Internet and more. But the first line of communication is the phone system. An on-hold communication network is one of the most cost-effective communication strategies, with a significant improvement in engaging callers, keeping them on the line longer, offering consistent branding, sales increases, and enhancing the overall client experience.

We know you are busy. As a business leader, you face daily meetings, deadlines, and other pressures. While you must actively direct your organization, you shouldn't have to get into the trenches yourself. That's why you hire experts.

You've worked hard to build your company's brand and public image. You understand that marketing is crucial. The telephone is your foremost point of contact with customers. When they are on hold, and they will be, it is the perfect time to tell them what's unique about your company—what sets you apart and what special promotions you may be offering. An audio production, properly done without platitudes such as "Thanks for holding" and "We appreciate your business," communicates what your company is about in a non-sales environment, so that you engage your callers and inform them rather than frustrate them.

You don't want to create another project to place on your desk. That is why you want a provider that will review your needs, research your company and industry to learn how you stand out from your competition, and produce the creative content that serves you best and reflects your brand.

You don't want to work with static technology such as CDs, MP3s and flash drives. You want a provider that delivers remotely and keeps your IT department out of the loop. This increases your turnaround time, and most importantly your staff is left to do what it does best.

You will find that most companies set their rates based on the number of changes you can make to your audio content over the course of a year. Our rate structure is based on the level of creative resources you need to portray your company as you wish it to be perceived. With Phone On-Hold® Marketing Systems, you can change your audio content as your marketing and advertising needs dictate.

Table of Contents

Mr. Bell's Enduring Invention

O ne of my finest hours was on the day I got rid of my BlackBerry. I remember the moment I decided it had to go.

Don't get me wrong: I love technology—that is, when it makes life simpler. Using it wisely to help businesses and their customers is what my company, Phone On-Hold® Marketing Systems, is all about. But my "smart" phone, it would seem, had ceased to serve.

Sitting at my desk, I had found a precious free moment to pause and reflect. I was admiring my collection of antique telephones, including two old crank magneto phones that reportedly came from the Swiss embassy. Winston Churchill once used them, I'm told. I'd had them restored.

What tale did those telephones tell? What words passed through those mouthpieces—what delights and despairs, what anguish and joys were communicated from afar? I have a 1913 Dictaphone that I'm trying to restore. In old movies, you can see secretaries using this early system. The secretary would toggle a switch to transfer the call to an executive in another room. On mine, a label under one switch says "Mr. Rogers." I wonder who he was?

Today, my office phone has fifteen lines. And as I sat in my reverie, several of them started flashing with incoming calls—a good thing for any business, of course, but at the same time my e-mail alert sounded, the interoffice chat window notified me that someone needed my attention, and someone was knocking at my door.

And then the cell phone joined in—or, rather, the "smart" phone, as these devices have somehow come to be known. Intelligence, as we know, is relative, and inhabits not only the mind but also the heart.

A few days later, on a rare family vacation, I was adjusting the sail on my boat. I could feel the swell of the waves. When dolphins jump and California sea lions bark, I feel at peace. As I squinted into the glint of sunshine on the water, I felt free—and then that amazing BlackBerry started buzzing, as if to say, "Come back, come back!"

The next day I found a Verizon store, walked up to the service counter, and set the thing down in front of the sales clerk.

"I can't stand this," I told him. "I don't want it anymore."

"Ah!" said he, gesturing toward a long row of models on display. "And I most certainly can understand why!" He picked one up. "Let me show you our Droid, the very latest platform …"

"No," I said. "You don't understand. I don't want this."

"Just wait till you see what this technology can do," he persisted. I started thinking about how long the learning curve would be to use this toy. He started tapping at menus and pinching at its screen, manipulating and magnifying the details of a digital world that, he said, offered something for everybody.

But not for me. It was just too much—far more information than I wanted; or rather, information that came at me without seeming to respect my time. It felt like what is known in the advertising world as an "interruptive cold call"—people who walk in without an appointment and expect you to devote half an hour to them, as if their time is more valuable than yours. What I wanted was to enjoy a simple sunset and the gentle ride over a two-foot swell with a 12-knot breeze—not the BlackBerry's cold call.

"I don't want this," I repeated to the salesman.

He seemed bewildered at my attitude.

"Look," I told him. "Let me show you how this relationship works: You're the salesman, I'm the customer. What's the most obvious question you should be asking me?"

He scratched his chin.

"Ask me what I want the phone to do," I said.

"Okay, what would you like the phone to do?" Ah! Maybe he's getting it!

"That's a good question!" I said. "I want to be able to make a call, and I want to be able to receive a call."

"Oh, yes, sir, you can do that, most certainly. And we have a texting package that will let you send…"

I repeated: "I want to receive a call. I want to make a call. That's it."

I know that young, techno-infused fellow didn't get what I was trying to say, but no matter. I was striking a blow for the cause of sanity. We are bombarded. We are under information assault. The average individual is hit with between 3,400 and 4,000 commercial impressions a day, in newspapers and on the radio, on highway signs and coffee mugs. Advertising is coming at us all the time. It has to be unique to engage you and get your attention.

I remember when prospective clients would be pleased to get a proposal in a few days by FedEx. These days, they expect it right away; sometimes they're calling me back, in fifteen minutes, to inform me: "I don't have it yet."

♦

"Mr. Watson, come here. I want to see you." That's all that Alexander Graham Bell chose to communicate in the world's first telephone call, in 1876, to his assistant who was in the next room. The first telephone call was a request for another human being to come closer. The new technology didn't push Mr. Watson away. Bell was appealing for a closer working relationship. The telephone was embarking upon its potential to become a means of connection, one on one, person to person.

The telephone is not going away, even in this time of digital diversity. It remains the ultimate tool for communication, which is fundamental to who we are.

The telephone is approaching a century and a half old. In this day and age, it seems a rather quaint, old-school device. But we can say with certainty that it's not going away, even in this time of digital diversity. The telephone remains the ultimate communication tool. The Internet and chat rooms are great, but we need to hear the inflections of another person's voice to truly communicate feeling and interest. The human need to communicate with another individual is fundamental to who we are. Only the technology of how we enhance our ability to do so will change, as our society and preferences and needs change. Think of it this way: The drive-in theater has faded away, but motion pictures are with us still.

When that first telephone call went out, the world changed. The telephone changed the way we communicate with one another in ways that the lowly telegraph, which had amazed the world thirty years earlier, could never do with the tappity-tap of its one-message-per-wire Morse code. No longer did you have to go down to the telegraph office to retrieve a message, or wait for its delivery. The language became real, and in real-time.

The telephone opened the door for our global economy. You might say it was the Internet of its day. It extended the neighborhood around the globe, through the many time zones and climates and terrains, and you could now talk—and do business—with those new neighbors swiftly and naturally. In colonial days, it took months to cross the sea between America and Europe. When the U.S. postal system was designed, delivery was on horseback, by Pony Express—amazing, in its day, but in this age of Outlook Express, we expect our mail ever faster.

The telephone certainly changed society from the outset, in ways simple and profound. A young man no longer had to shuffle up to a girl when he wanted to ask her out for a date—now he could ring her up on the phone, without even shaving first, and neither could see if the other blushed. But the telephone also opened the door to immediate and nuanced communication between heads of state. They could have transatlantic conversations without traveling months to meet. Outside of the computer chip, the telephone ranks as one of the most effective inventions that this planet has ever known.

If Alexander Graham Bell could see the mass communication of today's world, I think he'd want to know one thing: Is it bringing us closer together, or is it separating us?

One wonders what Bell would think if he could see all the ways his invention has been used. The telephone created the ability to talk, one on one, over many miles. Through the ensuing generations, we have learned to communicate with many people simultaneously and instantaneously, worldwide. That's the possibility that Bell's invention opened.

If that old Scotsman could visit us today and see the mass communication of today's world, I think he'd want to know one thing: Is it bringing us closer together, or is it separating us?

Technology should pull us closer and make our lives easier. Something is lost for those who choose to sit in dark rooms with glowing laptops and engage in chat rooms rather than head out to a party or meet a friend for lunch—perhaps one recently "friended," as they say in Facebookspeak. We tweet ourselves silly, thinking everyone cares. But something is gained, most undeniably, by the rise of the social networks, so long as they are used to enhance real relationships rather than replace them. They create the opportunity to form and renew bonds that otherwise might never take place. Many is the modern marriage that began with an online hello.

It has become so much easier to reconnect. A school buddy of mine called me recently, right out of the blue. I hadn't talked to him since the days we were in marching band together—we both played drums. It was a delight to hear from him, and we talked about what our old friends were up to now. We mused about wishing we could go back in time and offer some advice to the young people we once were.

At the heart of it all, you see, is our human longing for one-on-one connection where we can hear somebody's voice. All the technologies can enhance the communication experience, if used properly, but it's the telephone at the core.

Here's the secret to technological success: It must serve us, not consume us. The technology must be the catalyst for better relationships, whether personal or political or business. It must facilitate, not frustrate, those bonds. The goal is to make communication easier and more natural, not to make it irritating and robotic. When we experience the latter, it's time to reassess.

When you sit down in a conference room these days and take a look around, you'll see what I mean: So many people are unable to resist the urge to pull out their smartphones and check their e-mail and shoot off a text or two. Their minds never pause. Some will do this on the freeway at 70 miles an hour. It's insane. Comes a time when you want to remove yourself from that. So getting rid of that BlackBerry has simplified my life.

Used properly, the technology has fabulous potential. But for many people, it just sucks away the hours. How many times do you find yourself in your office answering e-mails all day? You feel as if you are working, but at the end of the day, what have you accomplished?

In an economy where people are trying to do more with less, they are finding that, when it comes to technology, they are doing less with more. Time is a valuable asset. When I'm talking to marketing people about the value of an on-hold communication network for their businesses, I reassure them that not only will it improve relationships with clients but also will save valuable time. We'll handle the details, I tell them; you reap the benefits. I generally hear a sigh of relief that I'm not suggesting another project to sit on their desk, waiting for them to implement.

Improving relationships, enhancing branding, saving time: That's what my clients are accomplishing. Some start out feeling that they'd rather not put anyone on hold, but that's because they have yet to see what a positive experience it can be. On-hold time presents the perfect opportunity to educate callers. It's all about communication and relationships and disseminating your company's image and building your brand. Do that first, and sales follow.

It seems ironic, but at Phone On-Hold® Marketing Systems, we're not about telephones foremost. We're about communicating well, saving time, improving relationships. We're about being people.

It seems ironic, I know—but even though our company is named Phone On-Hold® Marketing Systems, we're not about telephones foremost. We're about communicating well. We're about being people. As technology changes, we'll develop ways to put it to good use so businesses can deal better with their customers and with one another. That's what shows up on the bottom line.

Phones are crucial to a business's success when used effectively—they pull the customer closer. Used improperly, they can destroy a company's image, become an irritant, and push the customer away. This is why it is critical to train your staff and professionally manage your on-hold audio content.

The misuse of technology is nothing new. The early home telephones were arranged on party lines. One line would serve multiple residences, and you'd know whether the call was for you by the number of rings. Even today, a few people still are served by such systems.

Those were the days when the proverbial gossipy Mable would listen in on the line. You could never be assured of your privacy, and a loose tongue could spread your business about town in a flash. Mable would have loved Facebook, but she made do with what she had.

The operators, mostly women, sat at a big switchboard with patch cords, repeating: "Hello, to whom may I connect your call?" They would punch and move the cable, perhaps picking up a few tantalizing bits of gossip along the way.

Those old switchboards were the precursor for today's phone systems. They developed into what we call a key system unit, or KSU—basically, a computer made the switch instead of Mable. Along came bigger systems, such as the PBX, continuing through the decades to today's Voice-Over Internet Protocol, or VoIP, based on the Internet. It's a fascinating history.

And yet we're still worried that Mable is listening. Or maybe Big Brother.

Interactive mass media is the rage in today's marketing. But while businesses focus on websites, search engine optimization, and click-through rates, they must not lose sight of the original interactive platform—the telephone. Come what may, we'll always have the telephone. It will change in shape and feel and function. It will change in the means through which the voice is transmitted. But people will communicate, one to another, reaching out to get closer and build relationships personally and professionally, just as Alexander Graham Bell did in that first telephone call.

If Bell could see what we have now—all the blogging and twittering, chat rooms, texting and friending—he might observe that it's all quite wonderful but really it's just folks needing to talk to one another. It's all based on his telephone. It would be hard to blame him if he were to sue for royalties.

Knowing the fundamental role of the phone, what steps will you, as a business, take to make sure it is used to your advantage? Will you treat your customers with respect and demonstrate how you value their time, even when you place them on hold? Or will you greet them with a curt "Thanks for calling, please hold, *click*"—and deadly silence?

CHAPTER ONE

Getting
That Phone
to Ring

E verything that a company does in its marketing efforts—the ads, the promotions, the direct mail, the signs, community relations—is aimed at getting that telephone to ring. And once it rings, a company must take all the right steps to cultivate that new customer.

A caller's time on the business line could be a marketer's dream. Attracting the customer is what it's all about—but too often, a wonderful opportunity is wasted. It's amazing how much of that effort and expense goes for naught as the phone call, that supreme interactive exchange, is mishandled.

I recently called my mortgage company to pay a bill over the phone—and that's another use for the phone that has changed our lives—and the receptionist asked if she could put me on hold for a minute. She was, at least, polite about it; so many companies don't train staff to be courteous that way. But then I heard silence. Nothing. Not even the Captain and Tennille's greatest hits. I wasn't sure I still had a connection. And I was calling a huge corporation that must put countless people on hold every day. That's a lot of dead air, a lot of wasted opportunity.

On-hold time should be used to draw customers closer, not drive them away. Some businesses don't understand how important it is not to squander people's time. They miss the potential to build long-lasting relationships and as a result improve their bottom line.

Seventy percent of a company's callers typically are put on hold for thirty or forty seconds, according to a study from 1992—and by now, in this ever-more-manic world, that percentage likely has increased. The average person will be on hold 1.9 years in his or her lifetime, according to one estimate, and most of that time learns little about company images and brands.

It doesn't have to be that way. That time can be used productively to draw customers closer, not drive them away. But businesses, as a rule, don't see it. They don't understand how important it is not to squander their customers' time and their own potential to build long-lasting relationships and as a result improve their bottom line. They don't get it.

Would you turn your back on a customer that walks into your store for 30 to 40 seconds and ignore them? I think not, but that is what you are doing when your telephone and on-hold network skills are improper. That customer is likely to take his business to a place that offers prompt and courteous service. You may never see that customer again, nor his years of repeat business, nor the years of the business from his referrals.

Whether at the service counter or on the telephone, people on the front line are not trained properly on how to handle customers. They are burdened with the flood of phone calls and the parade of customers and repetitive questions and requests. Customers or clients are the whole reason for the business and its employees to exist, yet to an untrained staff they can seem like pesky annoyances. It's human nature: Many employees, when overworked, become less than friendly—unless they learn to like people!

Yet those callers might just want to ask a few questions before coming in. If they find your telephone etiquette lacking, I guarantee you they aren't going to take the time to visit your business or your website.

A friend was telling me that he called a floral shop in Cleveland and the florist was a bit grumpy. Maybe he felt overworked or was having a bad day, but he was curt and short on the phone and repeatedly was placing my friend on hold. My friend was trying to place a large order—but he finally ended up saying, "Look, never mind. Forget the whole order. I'm going to find someone who appreciates me." It's all about how you treat people—and that's a case where an on-hold communication network and proper training could have served the florist well. Placing people on hold is not a bad thing. The mistake is creating a poor and frustrating experience for them when you do.

Don't Waste a Prime Marketing Opportunity

I recently called the Department of Motor Vehicles to take care of a registration problem, and the recording advised me to call another number instead. I dutifully did so—and was advised that the DMV would be closed on July 5 as part of the Independence Day holiday—on the previous year.

Poor experiences like that leave callers frustrated. Your content must be kept current or you leave the feeling of getting the runaround. The caller is left with the impression that the business is sloppy, stagnant, overwrought, or maybe just doesn't give a damn.

Contributing to the problem has been the proliferation of off-shore call centers. If you're calling in for support from a software development company, for example, you could wait for what seems an eternity, and then you get an outsource person in a foreign country whose accent is hard to understand.

Many callers find it highly irritating when told "to speak English, press one." Why should a caller have to choose his country's predominant language? Yet many on-hold phone systems are set up that way, leaving a poor impression.

Companies usually just leave etiquette up to their IT department. What insanity is that? The IT people are not trained in marketing or advertising. They are not concerned about branding or image. They are low-voltage data people, concerned with how things work. They're more into what makes the machine tick than what makes people tick. They're good in their own field, but why let them determine a caller's first impression? I doubt your marketing department asks your IT department for counsel when designing brochures or creating advertising campaigns or branding strategies.

People are calling because they are interested in your business, for one reason or another. This is a prime point of opportunity. When the callers take the time to pick up the phone and dial, they are by definition interested in talking to you! They may have a complaint but more likely they want information, or they're considering your services or products.

That opportunity is a terrible thing to waste. Think of all the money that companies, collectively, spend to get the phone to ring— billions of dollars each year. And then they don't handle it properly. They throw that time away. Let's say you get fifty calls a day and half of them, twenty-five, go on hold for, say, thirty seconds. That's twelve and a half minutes a day. Then, let's say you're open the average of twenty days a month. That's 250 minutes. That's more than four hours that you could be speaking at little cost with callers who are interested in what you have to say.

A single sixty-second spot in Los Angeles could cost, depending on the station and day part, $2,500 to $3,000. And so much of that money is wasted because the commercials reach people who are simply not interested in your product or service. When you listen to a commercial for BMWs, do you rush right out to buy one? You may love BMWs, and the commercial indeed may get some people to check out what's for sale. But for the most part, if you're an off-road four-wheel-drive type of person, that commercial spot has been wasted on you. There is little chance you'll be buying a BMW. And even if you were to miraculously transform into a BMW lover, why would you not just shop at the closest dealer? What's so special about the one you see advertised?

When someone calls in to your company, he or she has you top-of-mind. This is no cold call—the caller is seeking you out, not vice versa. You have, on your phone line, a prospect who is primed to listen. Is this any time for silence? Yet often that caller is asked to "hold on" and hears nothing engaging. The caller feels his or her time is wasted and becomes irritated. In the caller's mind, you're just like all the others.

Imagine, instead, that the caller hears professionally crafted audio content that is designed to use his time wisely and effectively. The caller feels respected and appreciates hearing what the company has to offer. A good on-hold network provider will take time to learn about your business, your customers, your competition, your goals, and most importantly *what makes you different.*

Imagine that your callers hear a compelling description of your services and promotions—a different one highlighted each time they call. Imagine that those words are produced by experienced writers, voice-over actors, and technicians who customize the production just for you.

Imagine those things, and you'll see a *point of opportunity* you can't miss—and one that costs you little in comparison with conventional forms of advertising. Remember that conventional forms of advertising are designed as both a call to action and general institutional branding of your name. Because of the inherent waste in not reaching targeted customers, that budget line item for traditional media has to be significant. Not so with your *on-hold communication network.*

If you're a business that takes orders or reservations over the phone, such a communications network offers the perfect opportunity to inform and upsell. You can plant the idea in the callers' minds right at the time they are thinking about you, while your company is top of mind.

You want to build a relationship with callers, not raise their suspicions that you're just trying to sell them something. Your On-Hold Network is essentially a non-sales environment. On-hold time is a good opportunity to talk about who you are and demonstrate the passion, products and service the makes you different.

This isn't to say you should not deliver sales information whenever you have somebody waiting. The atmosphere may be ripe for marketing, but not an overt pitch—that would raise the old "door-to-door salesman" mentality in the mind of the caller.

This is a time to educate and inform. What you communicate in an on-hold network should reinforce your product, image, branding and reputation. If you run that BMW dealership, for example, you might talk about your passion for the business and how you got into it. You may talk about your commitment to great customer service and appreciation. You can reassure callers about the quality and integrity of your finance and service department. It's your opportunity to counter the prevailing belief that taking a car to the dealership for service is a costly mistake. Tell them you have all the parts, in stock and convenient, and you have the experts who work on engines just like theirs day in and day out. You might include things you have done for the community, the schools, your Little League sponsorship. Or tell the callers to be sure to say hello, when they come in, to Jennie Smith, your employee of the month. That builds relationships. Callers sense they are dealing with real people who care about their experience with your company.

How many times have you dialed the phone just to hear this: "Thanks for calling, please hold. We'll be with you in minute." Then comes inane music. Or silence.

Many companies don't understand why that's important. I was talking recently to a client, a pest-control company that's been around for a hundred years, literally. I'd heard a radio campaign in Los Angeles, and so I said, "Can you send me a copy of the radio commercial?" The client seemed confused: "What do you need that for? The campaign's designed to get people to call us, and what you do is for people who've already called us."

She was missing the point about what an on-hold network, with its creative abilities, can do for a company. What we want to do is engage the caller. A company should know the importance of creating an image and brand and building customer loyalty. The time a client is on hold presents an opportunity to do something creative. You don't want to sound like the company down the street. You want to give callers the feeling that they are dealing with genuine people who really want to serve.

Nonetheless, many companies still just turn their back on such potential business opportunity. The call comes in, and they blow it. They don't teach their employees how to answer the phone properly. They don't build the relationship. How many times have you dialed the phone just to hear this: "Thanks for calling, please hold. We'll be with you in minute." And then you hear simple music tracts. Or silence, interrupted by a receptionist saying they'll be with you when they can get to you.

Or, when a company does decide to make use of an on-hold network, it makes the mistake of launching into a brazen sales pitch, which can be counterproductive. In this environment, radio-style productions and hard sells do not work.

The Ice Cube and the Eskimo

"He's such a good salesman—he could sell an ice cube to an Eskimo." I've heard salespeople themselves use that line, almost as if they were proud of the deception. But that's not describing a good salesperson. That's describing a con man, who gives the many true salespeople a bad name.

I started my career in broadcasting and was always sales-oriented. I kept hearing the same comments over and over, ones that I'm sure you've heard many times as well: "He's about as trustworthy as a used-car salesman," and "They're just trying to sell me a bill of goods," and "I just can't stand those telemarketers."

Selling is far from a bad thing. It reflects how we can best be of service to one another. What is bad is a con man. An Eskimo does not need an ice cube.

For some reason, our society has come to perceive that salesmanship is bad. The truth is that without sales, the world as we know it would not exist. We erect a mental defense whenever we feel as if someone is trying to sell something to us that we don't need. That's why used-car dealerships, in the past, have developed a reputation that they cannot be trusted. And frankly it is true, because too many today try to sell rather than build a relationship. You don't have to talk people into buying. You just have to educate them on how you have a solution for what they need. If you're a wise salesperson and discover that you don't have the solution, you will send the customer to someone who does. The customer will deeply respect you for doing so.

If you've ever seen the movie *Miracle on 34th Street*, you may recall that Kris Kringle, although working for Macy's, sends shoppers to Gimbel's and other archrival department stores for toys that Macy's doesn't have. The customers are so impressed that they proclaim their enduring loyalty. Gimbel's, seeing that generosity of spirit actually pays off, adopts the same referral policy. The stores try to outdo each other. Both win by building relationships and trust.

Selling is far from a bad thing. For millions of years, salesmanship has advanced our quality of life as human beings having discovered how they can be of service to one another and what services will be most appreciated. If a country lacks an effective system of salesmanship, it risks impoverishment.

What is bad is a con man. An Eskimo does not need an ice cube, but an Eskimo might indeed need an igloo. Or a warmer coat. True salespeople endeavor to fulfill the customer's need, and they are involved in an honorable profession.

That's why here at Phone On-Hold® Marketing Systems, we first conduct what we call "discoveries" before attempting to offer any of our services. A lot of my colleagues in the industry do the same thing. BusinessVoice out of Toledo, Ohio; Commercials On Hold out of Atlanta, Georgia, and AMS out of Tampa, Florida, come to mind. Sometimes, we'll examine a prospect's situation and say, "You know what? There's nothing that you need from us." But often we find that we can help the customer immensely—and we both benefit.

Beware the IT Department

There are countless good salesmen in the field of on-hold communication, but seldom are the engineers and technicians who design the systems among them. They created, for example, the "auto-attendant," with which most everybody is familiar. That's the device that answers the phone and is supposed to be able to connect you to where you need to go. However more often than not you end up in a never-ending menu loop: "Thanks for calling," says a phone technician's voice. "Press 1 for sales, press 2 for service, press 3 for a staff directory, press 4 to repeat." Auto attendants aspire to efficiency, yet they are used in a way that can feel very distancing. The results are hardly people-oriented.

The problem is that the information technology professionals and the engineers who set up the systems are not salespeople. They're technical people, and they want to move the process along. They're not sensitive to people's reactions, and so what they create can irritate the caller. It breaks that relationship between business and customer.

There's nothing wrong with having an auto-attendant, but in setting up such systems it is important to heed a bit of advice we offer: "Don't go too deep, and don't go too wide." What that means is that you want to process the call quickly without giving the caller a multitude of choices. You also want to be sure the selection choices (the "CCR tree") actually take your callers to where they want to be. I know you have experienced the auto attendant that either does not give you the choice you are looking for or dumps you into a voice mail box after five minutes of navigating, whereupon you learn the department is closed. You also want to refrain from using the person in the office who thinks he or she has a great voice. This not only changes the perception of your company as being non-professional, but over time it will result in your auto-attendant turning into a hodgepodge of voices as employees come and go, leaving the image of your company seeming chaotic and unorganized. You want professional conversational voice actors whose voices match the company image you wish to project.

> Companies should have their marketing and salespeople work with us in setting up an on-hold network. They understand perception, image and branding. Technicians do not.

The reason that companies, when considering our type of service, often refer us to their IT technicians is that they are reacting by reflex when they hear the word "telephone," which the technicians install. These are talented people in their own realm, yes, but they are not marketing people. They are not into building relationships with clientele. They do, however, love new technology. I've seen many of them strap the latest telecommunication tool onto their belts like a Colt .45, as if warning others to "keep your hands off my network."

I have had clients lose out on many of the benefits that an on-hold provider can offer because they listened to their IT departments. But these are the people whom company executives often want us to work with the minute they hear the word "telephone." It's a knee-jerk reaction. Because those technicians aren't interested in marketing, what could have been a valuable initiative comes to a halt. The company never gets a grip on the need or a glimpse of the solution. And so it is left with a rudimentary device that spits out, "Thanks for holding." The company has lost the chance to build a dynamic relationship with customers and prospects.

Instead, companies should refer us to their marketing and sales department. They understand branding. They know their target market. In conventional advertising—television, radio, print, direct mail—they've proved themselves worthy. But the work doesn't stop there. The branding, loyalty and relationship building shouldn't just be part of the ad campaign. It needs to continue when the phone rings and through the customer interaction.

Too often, however, callers end up feeling mistreated and unappreciated, and once they do, any attempt to meet their needs is likely to raise that mental wall of resistance to being sold something. We want to help you keep that wall from rising. We want your callers to feel reassured that you are working hard to find solutions for what they need.

CHAPTER TWO

Our Industry and Its Image

When we start discussions with a potential client, we often find ourselves having to counter a prevailing myth. It's one that businesses cling to tenaciously: To deal effectively with customers, you must strive to never, ever put them on hold.

At risk of offending those very bright people who created the technology that has allowed on-hold networking to move in so many new and exciting directions, let me again point to the technicians who build and design the phone systems, and who developed the idea of the auto attendant. The caller endures a long and rambling menu, finally gets to the desired destination, and the system abruptly hangs up—"Thank you for calling, goodbye!"—followed by that diabolical dial tone.

It's similar to the fine mess you encounter on some amateur web pages. When websites first came out, they basically were just brochures. Today, building your own website is popular. Numerous companies try to make it seem simple. But you can't build your own website the way a professional can do it, making your site different than the others, attractive, with all the links working, and logically and conveniently arrayed. How many times do you go to a website and find out that it's "under construction"? What that tells you is the web designer doesn't know what he's doing or has been overcome by the time involved in doing it right. Or the website goes "too wide and too deep," losing sight of simplicity.

If a company gets a technician to create its website rather than a professional designer, the site is not only likely to fall short on design, but it may end up so complicated that it is difficult to find anything on it. That's the same sort of frustrating feeling that On-Hold Networks designed by technicians often leave with the caller.

Such ill-advised audio productions have conspired to create a negative image of the on-hold industry—and that's the image that's in the heads of our potential clients as we sit down with them.

> "I hate it when I get an automated machine," the shop owner told me. That's because his experience was with systems that did the job poorly.

We did a demonstration for a five-location pizza chain called Fresh Brothers Pizza, run by five brothers. Their product and their concept are phenomenal, and their business is growing and probably will be franchising. They were very impressed with our presentation, yet they still told us that they wanted live people answering the phone. They just would not hear otherwise. One of the brothers told me, "I hate it when I get an automated machine."

That's because his experience was with systems that did the job poorly, paid no attention to the personal and conversational approach, and ignored the very important marketing opportunity. People do not mind being "on hold" or having "automated answering services" if their experience is a good one.

What I believed would serve the brothers well was our product called the Call Handler Solution, which answers the phone and delivers a presentation of interest to callers—in this case, to customers calling in their orders. It shows a great return on investment.

"You know," I told the brothers when they expressed their skepticism about all such systems, "that's like me walking in here and saying I hate pizza, because I had pizza over at that other place and it was terrible." They at least listened to the presentation. I was even going to give them a few months to try out the system at no cost so that they could assess its potential. We created a demo for them, and one of the brothers called me back immediately to say he was impressed and would make sure the others listened to it.

The Call Handler's huge advantage is consistency, which is as crucial on the telephone as it is with any other marketing platform. An automated answering system ensures that the customer's immediate phone contact is cordial and commanding. A recorded greeting lets the customer know that he has called the right place and that his order will be taken promptly. Because the greeting is professionally recorded, the callers aren't subjected to the mumbling they often hear from live employees. That's especially important in this land of great diversity—and of many accents that can be hard to understand.

Heavy phone traffic necessitates customers being placed on hold. The Call Handler Solution deals with caller surges efficiently. Even if someone is available to take a call right away, an automated call handling system is still a superior means of answering the phone. It's light years ahead of having untrained, unmotivated personnel who flatly intone: "Would you like to try our double chocolate shake, okay how can I help you?"

Another pizza shop called Uncle Ernie's has used the service for many years now. The owner told us that one of his products featured on the Call Handler had a huge jump in weekly sales.

It brings us immense satisfaction to know that the services we offer are helping a good business do better than ever. But it's not uncommon for us to encounter a hard wall in the minds of business leaders who insist the job always should be handled by flesh and blood. The truth is, they are misguided. Properly designed, a professionally recorded system can convey the experience and image of a company long before a staff person deals with the call. It can even help the staff person be more efficient. A good system enhances the human role exponentially and creates a positive caller experience.

Don't Annoy Your Customers

When the on-hold industry started in the early 1980s, it was common for companies to use platitudes such as "Thank you for holding" or "We appreciate your business." As we have seen, that was because many people who were creating the audio files were either telephone technicians or out-of-work disc jockeys, unschooled in advertising and marketing and simply unsophisticated. After all, the industry was in its infancy.

It's now known that platitudes and apologetics such as "thanks for holding" or "we're sorry you have to wait" are actually perceived by callers as irritants and insincere. Their subconscious—or all-too-conscious—reaction to the first comment is likely to be, "Yeah, right"; and to the latter, "Don't rub it in."

Through the years, we have learned these lessons:

- Never remind callers that they are on hold. Rather, supply them with quality information that will keep them attentive. That way, the time will pass more quickly.

- Never play commercial jingles. The on-hold network is not the media for this. Callers do not perceive this as a sales environment. The average person, remember, is hit with over 4,000 commercial impressions a day. Conventional advertising channels have to reach out and grab the attention of the consumer. That's not the case with an on-hold network: You can have a one-on-one communication experience with someone who you know is interested in you. So you don't have to shout. You just have to inform.

- Do not play recognizable music because the caller will then begin to listen to the song and pay less attention to you.

- Most importantly, don't pack too much information into your copy. This rushes the voice-over actor and takes away from the delivery. It is much better to change the content often than it is to try to pack every bit of information into one production.

Early in my career, I started seeing how people used the phone. A receptionist with five lines answers by saying, "Thanks for calling, please hold." That's a terrible experience. It's also a typical experience. And to make matters worse, as a caller waits on hold and becomes increasingly frustrated, a recorded voice reminds him that he's waiting and tries to apologize.

Still, we have clients today who insist we put the "thanks for holding" line on their system. They just don't understand. They figure they're being polite. We give them what they want, but we do advise them that their callers would be hearing just what they expected to hear and nothing about what sets the company apart from its competition. In other words, the company will sound and be perceived just like everyone else.

Words of appreciation strike callers as mere conversation crutches—sort of the way "hey, how're you doing?" come across from someone in an elevator. Those are just chatter words without real meaning. You respond "fine," even if you're far from fine, because you recognize the insincerity. Or a colleague may say, "So, how's business?," not particularly interested in the details of your quarterly report. Those are reflex words. And that's how a caller on hold perceives expressions of appreciation—as reflex words, hollow, just passing time. They remind callers that they're waiting and seem to communicate that you really are not interested in them.

It's known now that platitudes and apologetics such as "thanks for holding" or "we're sorry you have to wait" are actually perceived by callers as irritants and insincere.

Worse, some companies, in creating their on-hold production content, actually apologize to the caller for having to hold. That's the worst thing an On-Hold Network can do. It sounds as if you're acknowledging that you have a persistent problem, and the words can come across as: "We know we have to make you wait because we aren't adequately staffed to deal with you and, besides, somebody else is more important than you are."

An Israeli study, published in 2007 in the *Journal of Applied Psychology*, examined the effects of apologizing to callers. Findings suggested that apologies can irritate callers and make them feel they are making no real progress toward being served.

It's better to spend the time educating and informing your callers. After all, they are on your phone line, and your communication network. They are interested in you.

It's All In the Approach

When we work with a company on setting up a telephone communications network, one thing we ask is how much training the company does for its staff—particularly, whether the staff is trained on how to answer the phone. Unfortunately, the answer often is none. "It's not in the budget" is what we hear. Or not enough time.

It's counterproductive, however, to spend all that money getting the phone to ring but not spend the money and time to train the staff on how to deal with customers once they do call. Companies need to educate employees on answering the phone. Too often, staff members don't answer the same way every time. They lose the sense that they're there for the customer—not that the customer is there for them.

If you call my office, you will always hear the phone answered the same way, every single time. And you will virtually always hear the same voice. We know that such consistency helps our customers feel comfortable with us and know what to expect when they call our office.

When I was leaving my career in broadcasting for new opportunities, I prayed: "I want to continue to use my voice somehow." That prayer and that ambition gave me the courage to take my company, Phone On-Hold® Marketing Systems, full time. I also worked as a voice-over actor, and I do so to this day as a member of the Screen Actors Guild. Although I don't do much of the recording myself anymore for Phone On-Hold®, I hire others to do so.

If you call my office, you will always hear the phone answered the same way, and virtually always the same voice. Consistency helps our customers feel comfortable with us.

What I've learned is that how you speak to people really affects their mood. Sometimes, even in my own office, I'll hear: "So and so's on the phone, and he's really mad." I get on the phone with that caller and find someone quite pleasant. It all depends on how you treat people. It's all in the approach.

There's so much power behind speaking softly and saying, "You know what? Let me help you with this." It's that old principle of martial arts—if a blow is coming to you and you resist it, you have two forces opposed. What you need to do is receive the energy and direct it past you, not create resistance. It's similar with the spoken word. When I need to talk with an employee about a problem, I first say with a soft and clear inflection, "Look, we're solution-oriented here. Let's not get defensive. You must have a frustration, so let's build a system to fix it together"—and that takes the heat out of the room. The employee feels respected and heard.

Broadcasting norms and expectations have changed, in recognition of a softer approach. In the world I grew up in, the traditional "announcer" voice, with the Gary Owens type of delivery, sold products. On radio and television today, advertisers are looking for a conversational, soft-sounding actor who communicates a genuine relationship to the listener.

Two master orators were Presidents John F. Kennedy and Ronald Reagan. Their approaches differed greatly, yet each commanded the spoken word and communicated passion. Kennedy came across with the forceful energy of the day. You knew he was solid. Reagan took a soft-spoken approach. His words made you feel he was coming from a place of wisdom. He spoke slowly and projected great thought and leadership.

I spent a lot of time listening to Reagan and the way he crafted his words. I was fortunate to be chosen to be the voice-over actor for walking tours at the Ronald Reagan Library in Simi Valley, California. If you go there and step on Air Force One, you'll hear me welcome you aboard. At the library, I saw some of his incredible letters and realized his great command of the language. Every word had a reason to be there, and his vocal delivery emanated feeling for every word he had written. Reagan's approach wasn't complicated. It was real. It's the same approach your on-hold network needs.

Kennedy was in a different world, in the middle of the Cold War, dealing with the tension of the Bay of Pigs and needing to energize the American people. His ability to deliver his passion effectively came across each time he spoke, especially in his famous speech challenging us to land a man on the moon by the end of the decade. You believed him. It was all in his delivery.

Whether one is leading a nation or a company, it's crucially important to maintain a presence and maintain consistency. As a business leader, you need to ensure that your staff members maintain that consistent image and delivery over your telecommunication system. It's your communication channel, so use it wisely.

Callers want to feel a company cares about them. They want respect, and when they get it, they'll take your products or services seriously.

Michael E. Gerber, in his book *The E-myth*, tells a story that goes something like this: A tired driver stops at a motel nestled among the trees. The gentleman at the counter says, "Good evening, sir" and "How may I help you?" He asks the traveler which paper he reads and his favorite drink. After a bellboy escorts him to his room, the *Wall Street Journal* arrives in ten minutes. Hungry, he goes to the lounge, where the maitre d' informs him his Scotch is waiting at the bar.

If you were that man, would you go back to that motel?

A year later, he does go back. He's brought a friend with him to show how great the place is, but the proprietor recently sold it. Nobody's at the front desk. No bellboy. Finally, a woman peers out from a lobby door and says, "What do you want?"

How would you feel now, with expectations dashed? Would you ever return?

The key is consistency. Even if your motel is not top-class, customers will return for consistently good service. Even if you don't make the best hamburger, customers will come back knowing they'll get the same decent food each time. Whatever your business, consistency sells—and your telecommunications system should reflect that truth.

Your telephones are your direct, targeted channel to clients and customers. They need to know what to expect every time they call you. What they expect is respect, and when they get it they will take you seriously and talk favorably about you to others. That's why your phone system needs to be first and foremost under your control and part of your marketing strategy.

Your receptionists and IT personnel may lack the training and vocal delivery for consistent customer service. Few things thwart good communication faster than abuse of the spoken word and carelessness in how it's delivered. Poorly trained staff and poorly designed On-Hold Networks contribute to the myth that customers must never be placed on hold.

We recently began working with a company with 450 locations nationwide that wanted a new on-hold services provider. The provider it had been using was delivering inconsistent, unsatisfactory service, sometimes failing to return calls. Out of fifteen competitors, the company chose Phone On-Hold® Marketing. I had sent its representative a message praising its proposal request as "well-thought-out, well constructed, direct, to the point—you know what you're looking for. I can bring solutions to this. Good job, whether you use us or not."

That communicated that we valued the company's interest in us and above all respected its needs. Even when we lose deals, I send out coffee mugs stuffed with counter candy and say, "Thanks for the opportunity." You never know when a prospect may return to do business with you—or recommend you to others. Caring about people comes back to you tenfold. It's all in the approach.

Our Industry Association

There's an inertia in the way things always have been done. A lot of businesses, when looking for an on-hold service provider, believe they just need sound and music, and they go to companies such as Muzak, DMX, and Mood Media, who at the time of this writing had bought out Muzak, as they were experiencing financial problems.

But an effective on-hold network involves so much more than just the sound, and far more than simple messages—though music and messages once were the focus, as evidenced by the name our industry group still uses, the On-Hold Messaging Association. Over the years, providers who stay on the cutting edge have come to understand that it is not about just "thanks for holding, be with you in a minute." It is about engaging callers to listen attentively while they are thinking about your company.

At Phone On-Hold® Marketing Systems, we now avoid the word "messaging" because it doesn't communicate the breadth and effectiveness of what we do. We're competing against companies that don't understand the value of what they could do. They connect a message or song to the phone system port and they're done. And to make matters worse, that's what a lot of businesses believe they want. They don't see the value of their telephone system as a communication channel—one that is more valuable, I would argue, than the traditional advertising channels.

We now avoid the word "messaging" because it doesn't communicate the breadth and effectiveness of what we do.

The misperception could be the fault of the industry itself because, in the beginning, providers all called it "on-hold messaging" or "messaging on hold." It was the nature of the business. But "message" implies voice mail. What we provide is really a network channel for talking to your clients right at the time they're thinking about you. Why would anyone throw that opportunity away? Yet few companies make good use of the potential, including Fortune 500 firms such as Verizon and AT&T and others.

You use an on-hold network to reach customers and clients— just as you would over a radio station, television, or with print or direct mail. But this is a channel you own that communicates with callers just when you are the main focus on their minds. If you're a pet supply company, for example, you can be fairly certain the caller has a pet. There's no advertising waste. You don't spend money reaching people who couldn't care less.

Some companies, such as Costco Wholesale, do understand the importance of engaging their callers, and their marketing departments drive the audio content of their on-hold networks. Companies that "get it" know that callers have better uses for their time than listening to music or beeps—or silence. The last thing they want to do is irritate potential customers. It's a lesson worth repeating: If you ran a retail store and a customer walked in, would you turn your back on him or her for forty seconds? How do you think that customer would feel? And how he would describe his experience with others?

A well-designed on-hold network helps to ensure your callers stay with you. Because they've come to expect that their time on hold will be wasted, they turn their thoughts elsewhere—sort of the way people get up and run to the refrigerator during a TV commercial. People want to make the most of their time, so if you engage them with valuable information and entertainment, you'll stay "top of mind" while they wait.

Put yourself in the caller's shoes: You dial a car dealership and get placed on hold. As a busy person, you start attending to other tasks—reading a report, checking your schedule, or just surfing the Internet. You're not thinking about the dealership anymore. You're not thinking about the new models coming out, or services available, and certainly not about the company culture. But you could be.

Even if the caller just wanted to make a service appointment, the dealership could have used the on-hold time to educate and enhance the caller's experience. Often, businesses put up informational signs around the shop; if they find that worthwhile, why not impart the same information to clientele before they enter?

A professional provider can create a production that truly engages the caller. For example, a business could have a production that sounds like a radio talk show in which the principal of the company talks about how he got involved in the industry, his passion for customer service, and his community activities. That is the type of content that engages the caller.

Many members of OHMA, the On-Hold Messaging Association, know full well the value of what they do: They put time and energy into helping their clients sound different from their competitors.

Many providers in our industry do know the value of the service they bring to their clients. They put time and thought into developing the right creative approach to make a business sound different from its competitors.

As a member of OHMA, which I helped to found in 2000, we are a part of an international organization composed of audio marketing agencies that have joined together for several common purposes. We strive to advance the business community's awareness of on-hold services as a cost-effective marketing and communication tool. We set and maintain high service and ethics standards, share ideas and technologies, and provide members with networking opportunities. To be a part of the association, you have to be in business for at least five years, and more than half your revenue has to come from providing an on-hold communication network.

With my background in radio broadcasting, I had seen fellow broadcasters join together in industry associations. We would get together and talk about formatting problems and overcoming other competitive advertising channels such as television and print. We would share ideas and concepts and strategies. Though we bid against one another for ad dollars, we were still comrades in the industry.

But when I moved into the field of on-hold networking, there was no one to talk to. It was as if everyone thought what they were doing was a secret. For example, when I talked to manufacturers of digital players and asked for names of others they were dealing with, they acted as if they feared their ideas would be stolen. In that kind of climate, without discussion and sharing, undesirable practices can develop in any industry.

Finally, in the mid-1990s, I got in touch with David Hearld of Profit-Tell International in Illinois, and we started sharing information and asking questions. We realized some small-minded on-hold providers had been trying to find out how much their competitors were charging by calling and posing as potential clients—quite a waste of time. It showed how unsophisticated many of the providers were.

If I found that I was being "shopped" by a competitor, I'd be straightforward: "Why don't you just ask me?" I'd say. "I don't mind telling you what I charge. What are you afraid of?" If they told me their own rates, I'd suggest their services were more valuable than that. They just did not understand the impact they could have on a business.

Those of us who were looking to grow were identifying target markets, implementing best business practices, designing business plans, and creating strategic objectives. In 2000, the owners of six small on-hold companies met in Florida and began what would soon become OHMA. They met in the office of Mike Edwards, owner of On Hold Technologies. I received a call from my manufacturer representative at the time, Todd Griffin at Premier Technologies in Long Lake, Minnesota. He told me about that meeting of minds, something I had talked about for years. The six of them shared ideas, and I started reaching out to them and others; finally, eighteen of us had our first conference, in New Orleans.

Our hope was to collaborate and build a better perception of on-hold communication. The industry was young—it started in the early '80s—and many of those involved had a technical background and very little advertising and marketing vision. We defined OHMA's purpose and policies: primarily, to develop good business practices and education within the industry. We wanted to create standards, teach providers the true value of what they were doing, and help them articulate the importance of this communication channel.

Cheap isn't better. Those who think it is are buying into the IT mindset that just sells equipment.

Most providers would cut their rate the moment a prospect balked at it. But cheap isn't better. Often they were thinking about simply delivering sound rather than enhancing the client's image. We urged them to offer services not on the basis of price but rather on their marketing and branding value. Too much emphasis on price was creating a perception that this creative telecommunication channel was just a place to put sound and "thanks for holding" messages so the caller would know the line was still connected. In truth, no traditional advertising channel can deliver as much value for the money as an on-hold network.

The association also policed itself with regard to solid business practices and ethics. We've had some issues in the past. One on-hold provider sold a major client a third-party lease and then jumped ship. He wasn't there to build the information and create productions, service equipment, or anything that he promised, yet the client was on the hook to the third party for a three-year lease—with no content for an on-hold network. The company turned to us at the time. It had been sold the service at a low rate of $25 a month, but I explained that level of service should come closer to $60 a month, as they were a large multi-location account. However, I agreed to let the company subtract the $25 from my rate for the remaining year and a half it had on its lease, then pay the full rate.

That company has been a client of Phone On-Hold® Marketing for years now. We worked with its marketing staff, reviewed its needs, and provided the service it deserved. The lesson: Companies should make sure they are hiring a bona fide on-hold provider.

OHMA has been demonstrating to trade groups that we are a serious industry that plays a key role in business telecommunications.

As the industry association has grown, we have evolved from meeting in a room to getting together annually in Las Vegas, Atlanta, San Diego, St. Louis, and other areas of the country. We have been working to help companies pool some resources and demonstrate to trade groups that we are a serious industry that plays a key role in business telecommunications.

We're broadening our scope. We have had international involvement from England, Singapore, Australia, and Canada. And when I served as chairman of the association, I worked with Rick Welsh of On Hold Marketing Services on the idea of joining our conference with the IBMA, the International Business Music Association, providers of music overhead and sound systems for businesses. The goal was to build relationships and foster networking among providers.

The power of networking, after all, is the foundation of what on-hold companies provide to their clients—so the providers certainly should see the value in networking effectively with one another.

CHAPTER THREE

A World
of
Difference

T he ocean was my first love—and in many ways, it still is. I
wanted to grow up to be a naval architect, and I used to spend
hours in my room designing boats. Then I decided I would
become an oceanographer who would design underwater cities in
the Sea of Cortez, because it was such a pristine habitat, and create
fish farms to solve world hunger. Jacques Cousteau was my boyhood
hero. To this day I have a passion for the sea and sailing—and for
adventure and discovery.

My father, Cmdr.
Joseph F. Turpel, was a
hard-hat diver for the Navy
and went on to the top ranks
in the service before retiring
in 1971. When I was young,
I wanted badly to have some
scuba gear of my own. My
father offered to match every

cent I could save from working on my paper route. And I finally got my equipment. I must have raised all of sixty dollars, and he matched it, and we went together to the Navy dive outlet where real professionals helped me put my gear together. I received my certification when I was only 14 years old, which was unheard of at the time.

> **My father's spirit of caring has influenced me for a lifetime and is reflected in what makes our company different from its many competitors.**

I'm proud to have had that sense of ingenuity instilled in me, at such a young age—the spirit of making my own money and negotiating an investment proposition. As a military family, we moved frequently, so I became very sociable. I think that was a way of adapting to ever-changing environments: I had to adjust to new friends, new ideas, new expectations, and move easily among the various cliques that every child comes to know so well, trying to fit in. I focused on developing solid, meaningful, lasting relationships. That ability to adapt and to deal with people of all stripes has served me well, I believe, in my career.

My father gave me abundant encouragement. He showed me a spirit of caring and respect for oneself that I know has influenced me for a lifetime. My dad lived the Shakespearean line, "This above all: to thine own self be true." I hope that I have come to live those words half as much as he did. I believe his example is reflected in what makes our company different from many of our competitors.

Our Focus on Relationships, Branding and Image

Phone On-Hold® Marketing Systems emphasizes the relationship between the business and its customers—and that's a focus you won't find in many of our competitors. Companies spend hundreds and thousands of dollars—as an industry, billions—on advertising as they try to create a statement of who they are. That's a lot of creative energy, time and expense, and the momentum shouldn't stop after the phone finally rings. Through an on-hold networking channel, we want to help our clients maintain and reinforce that image.

One of our first tasks is to educate the company about the fundamental need to identify itself precisely for the consumer—and how it can reinforce that identity through its phone system. An on-hold network is a very intimate approach: It's an opportunity to talk one-on-one to the prospect, customer or client. Unfortunately, too often the caller hears radio commercials, or gets placed on hold to hear nothing but beeps.

I know a car dealership that sells high-end vehicles—Cadillacs, Land Rovers and the like, where image is crucial to sales and customer service. But all that dealership wants is music on the phone line. It plays a loop of classical music that it thinks makes it sound sophisticated. The general manager simply wants sound: After all, he himself has long been accustomed to hearing the typical "thanks for holding, be with you in a moment." Instead, that dealer could be communicating with potential and repeat buyers. Why should they come on in now, instead of visiting the competitor down the road? He should educate his customers about what makes his dealership different.

> Our tag line is "IMAGINE a better way to CONNECT." That's the whole point: Don't settle for the impersonal. You can "connect" in ways that solidify your business relationships—and improve your bottom line.

In illustrating the importance of our services to prospective clients, I point out how an On-Hold Network would be in their own best interest. "I'm not going to sell you," I say, "but you need to pay attention to this. You can get a lot more credibility through what we offer than from what some out-of-work disc jockey will come up with in his garage." Then I point out the waste in traditional forms of advertising: Even if a direct-mail campaign has a 2 percent return, the rest of the effort was wasted on people who didn't care. But when you have a caller on the line, you know that person is interested already.

Phone On-Hold's® original tag line was "communicating one-on-one," an appropriate emphasis in this technological age when face-to-face time with others has declined dramatically. It's a void we help fill with a communication handshake that comes much closer to face-to-face than the impersonal approach so many companies use. Today, our tag line is "IMAGINE a better way to CONNECT." That's the whole point: Don't settle for the impersonal. You can "connect" in ways that solidify your business relationships—and improve your bottom line.

How We Learn About Our Clients

To help a new client, we first need to learn about the company culture. We provide a discovery sheet, which can be filled out over the phone or in person, on which we ask basic questions: Do you have any promotions? Do you have any seasonal aspects to your business? Who is your ideal customer? Who are the people who are calling you? Do you have a lot of repeat callers? How much phone traffic do you have?

We need to know. The approach will be different for a client getting a hundred calls an hour, vs. ten calls an hour. They both need to utilize their on-hold network, but with a different creative approach. Call volume helps determine how active you need to be when changing your audio content and of course it can also determine the length of the production. Your marketing landscape and planning also come into play to determine how you direct the updating of your audio content. Repeat callers are important to consider as well.

We do a lot of work in the medical field. I have had some doctor groups mention that their patients only call every six months or so. Those patients shouldn't hear the same message six months apart. That makes a business sound stagnant. The On-Hold Network could be talking about so much else.

We also want to know how much training the company does for its staff—particularly, on how to answer the phone. Unfortunately, the answer often is none. Business owners get busy, and they just don't understand how important telephone etiquette is. I recommend Nancy Friedman's book *The Telephone Doctor* for an eye-opening discussion of the subject.

> In our Client Needs Analysis, we dig for details about a company so that we can assist in maintain the image and brand that it has worked so hard to develop.

We went through a discovery with Hyatt Hotels, which was redesigning its auto attendants and wanted to match its brand with the right voice. Assessing their needs, we came up a menu that worked efficiently. We considered what I know to be true about auto attendants: An effective delivery cannot run "too wide and too deep" but should be thoughtfully designed and easy to navigate. When we sent back a quote, we also rewrote the script with a note of how our revision would better position the company, and why. Hyatt encompasses three major brands: the Hyatt, the Hyatt Regency, and the Hyatt Park Plaza—different experiences and perceptions that needed to be communicated to their guests. However the rules of communication are consistent, and through focused discovery we found the clues for a more effective menu.

In our Client Needs Analysis, we dig for details about a company so that we can deliver an engaging production that will provide a positive experience for the caller. The analysis has several sections, including a business profile, a marketing profile, and a profile of the company's callers. We learn about the company's business focus and how much it emphasizes customer service.

Statistics show that 85 percent of American small businesses fail. In *The E-Myth*, Gerber points out that technicians, not entrepreneurs, start most businesses. Entrepreneurs have visions, but it's the technicians, who know how to do the work, who set the business up.

But they don't pay attention to how it should be run—and thus the high failure rate.

Let's say I make a really cool widget and the word spreads, my reputation grows, and orders pour in. I find myself so busy working in the business that I can't work on the business. Quality control suffers—as does customer service, because I just can't do it.

With the discovery and Client Needs Analysis, we learn about situations like that. In essence, the analysis tells us what the company thinks of itself. It's clear right away whether any thought has been given to answering the questions. If we determine that the company truly is branding itself, we can develop on-hold content accordingly. But if we run into people who can't answer those questions, then we have to do something different for them. We may even have to help create their concept of who they are as a business so that they can communicate that to their callers.

By learning about the company in this manner, we can present our plan for how we could help it. We need, first, to educate: The company must understand that an on-hold network is a powerful tool and an affordable one.

A Vision of Something Different

One day in 1984, as I was working at a radio station in Thousand Oaks, California, my telephone rang. It was a friend of mine, a client of the station who owned a pool-supply store, and he had an idea.

"I want you to come down and put the radio station on my phone system," he said, "so when I put people on hold, they can hear something instead of silence—they can listen to the radio."

Interesting idea, I thought. But I knew that playing the radio station wouldn't be wise. For one thing, callers on hold might hear advertisements from his competitors. But the big problem was that it wasn't a legitimate thing to do: Radio stations must pay royalties to performers for the songs they air, through groups such as ASCAP, BMI and SESAC. Rebroadcasting that signal onto any public system, including a company's on-hold network, can be considered a rebroadcast and is subject to royalty payments to the artists. Bottom line is: If you want to play, you have to pay. The risk is real: Business owners who play copyrighted material on their on-hold networks have lost many cases in court. A professional on-hold content provider will be offering and covering the music license fees for you.

I told my friend that I had a better idea, something different: "Instead of playing the radio station, why don't I make an advertisement about you?" It would be a licensed tape that he could play on his on-hold network.

> **I told a friend who ran a pool supply store that I had a better idea, something different, for his callers: "Instead of playing the radio station, why don't I make an advertisement about you?" And Phone On-Hold® Marketing was born.**

So that's how it started. His friends heard it, and his friends' friends heard it, and they, too, requested tapes. Phone On-Hold® Marketing was born. I kept my radio job and ran my new business part time. From my contacts in the broadcasting business, I was able to assemble a network of voice-over actors to do vocal recordings.

I had been involved in radio since my college days at Mississippi State University. Our family always lived near the ocean—Hawaii, California, the Gulf Coast when I was growing up—and that no doubt contributed to my youthful interest in oceanography. So as a young man, I entered college intent on becoming a civil engineer.

I got involved in the college radio station for various reasons. One was my social nature, which was a good fit with broadcasting—as was my vocal quality that seemed to lend itself to on-air announcing and voice-overs. During summer vacation, I went down to Biloxi and worked part time at WLOX and eventually I was hired commercially at WSSO in Starkville, Mississippi, when I returned to college there.

Radio work fascinated me, and, let's face it, it was fun. As a 19-year-old with visions of grandeur, I switched my major to business, then dropped out of school and headed for California with ideas of becoming some big radio guy and an actor.

And I did work in radio, for about eighteen years, on the air for about twelve of those years—I was a disc jockey, spinning the top forty—and, for the last six, in management and sales. You bounced from radio station to radio station back then, and I found myself working at Thousand Oaks KNJO 92.7 FM and at KMDY Comedy Radio, the longest-lasting all-comedy radio station in the country. It was during that time that I started Phone On-Hold® Marketing Systems, identifying a growing need for such service.

As a 19-year-old with visions of grandeur, I headed for California with ideas of becoming some big radio guy and an actor. I worked in radio for about eighteen years, as a disc jockey, and then in management and sales.

About that time I began working for the Children's Radio Network in Los Angeles, feeling frustrated with the changes taking place in the broadcasting industry, with companies such as Viacom and Cumulus gobbling up radio stations. When I moved into the Ventura County market, there were seventeen radio station owners, and now there are just a few. The whole format had changed.

One day I was sitting in my office, with a large window overlooking the L.A. skyline. I was at a big oak desk, with a big oak credenza behind me, and a big oak bookcase in front of me with somebody else's books in it—the previous occupant had left without taking his belongings. And I called my wife and I said, "I can't stand this anymore."

I quit the next day. I walked into the little office that I used for Phone On-Hold® and started dialing like crazy. It was exciting. But I was scared that I was going to fail. That's what stops everyone in their tracks. I had kids, a wife, a mortgage.

And then it just clicked. My Uncle Al, who recently passed away, used to tell me, in his Boston accent: "Oh don't worry, Peter; you're going to be fine." My mother tells me I'm a lot like her dad, my grandfather. He'd often worry about how he was going to get through the day, but he managed to keep a real estate company going right through the Great Depression. He came across as a worrier, but he certainly must have known how to get things done. I take heart in that, because for all the worries we have day by day, it's the big picture that really matters.

That was August of 1993, when I took the business full time. The rest is history. I networked, and I stayed involved in the community, which gave me visibility. Business picked up, and in the years since we've built up clients nationwide and in Canada and Puerto Rico

My office is in Newbury Park, California, but I started in my closet, actually, while I was still in broadcasting, and then I built a studio in my garage and rented an office down the back hallway from the radio station. In 1995, two years after taking the business full time, we moved to the only four-story building in town, with an office of about 600 square feet, and later to one on the same floor that was about 1,400 square feet. Then we moved into another building where I'm at today—the old Wilson Sporting Goods plant where golf clubs once were made. We have about 2,600 square feet now, with two recording studios.

Life was difficult and exciting in other ways: I had custody of my children when they were growing up, since Hayley was 3 and Christopher was 7. It was the worst time in my life and the best. It was a very painful time, but I made a list of all the things I wanted to do. I started bicycling and running. I started sailing again, and scuba diving, and skiing.

I even tried skydiving. I've jumped out of airplanes twice. It's an amazing experience. The first time was a sunset drop from a DC-3. I pulled the chute at 5,000 feet and saw the sunset behind Catalina Island, a hundred miles away. The second time was out of a little Cessna 172. It's quite a rush to climb out on an airplane wing and hang on at 10,000 feet, then just let go.

Then I was fortunate to meet my second wife, Michelle. She helped raised the little ones, and we had two more—Brianna and Anthony.

In the early days of Phone On-Hold®, I'd often bring the kids into the office and put them in sleeping bags so that I could work at night. What they probably remember most about those office visits was the milk and chocolate chip cookies. It was fun. Even during those rough times, I have great memories of raising a family, building a business, looking for adventure.

Today I have ten regular staffers. That includes voice-over engineers who work in the office on a regular basis, but we have others whom we bring in for different needs. And those needs can be quite diverse. For example, recently I needed a Japanese script for a high-end hotel. I can't keep a Japanese guy on staff, of course, so we put out a casting call. And I remember the first Spanish script I ever did. I did the voice-over myself, and I don't speak Spanish. I wrote the script in English, and a friend who was teaching Spanish at Oxnard College translated it into Spanish for me and recorded it. Then I repeated the whole production phonetically. I had no idea what I was saying, but it worked. The client was very pleased.

Such is a day in the life of an on-hold network producer.

Though I left broadcasting, I entered a business that still allowed me to use my voice acting skills—and to be creative. That creative drive has been part of my heart and soul since childhood. Even before I dreamed of being an oceanographer, I wanted to be an actor. I told my parents about it when I was in fourth grade. "You can't be an actor," they said. "You've got to be a postman." That was typical and understandable thinking among those who had endured the Depression.

Though I left broadcasting, I entered a business that still allowed me to use my voice—and to be creative. That creative drive has been part of my heart and soul since childhood.

Even when I was in my 20s and working in broadcasting, I still had this longing to get into acting, so I took classes and got an agent. I still have the old composites: Agents would assemble pictures and information to distribute to the producers and casting directors. I started taking voice-over classes and workshops, hoping to do commercials. The trend, continuing today, was toward natural voices from people who seemed real. No longer was the traditional "announcer voice" in vogue all the time.

I got a couple of breaks. The biggest was for the 2001 Honda Accord, with commercials running in seven regions around the country. My favorite television voice over was a spot created by Ruben, Postaer and Associates out of Santa Monica, California; Jon Yarbrough producer, where a man driving his Honda to see his girl-friend, with a big sign on top of the car saying, "Will you marry me?" Then I came on with the voice-over. What I liked most about it was the feeling of reaching out creatively to others—the "people" experience.

In my career, I've been able to combine my various interests and natures: my creative side, my interest in science and technology, and my social side. To make it all work, I have needed one more important element: the willingness to take a risk. That's what makes things happen.

I exhibited that spirit of adventure early with my interest in oceanography and diving. Back in school, when the teacher would ask, "What do you want to be when you grow up?," the other kids would say "policeman" or "fireman"—but I was saying "archaeologist."

In my career, I've combined my interests and natures: my creative side, my interest in science and technology, my social side. And one more important element: the willingness to take a risk.

That sense of discovery relates to what I do now in my business. I like to think I'm doing something similar to what the early inventors were doing. I'm dealing with technology they couldn't have dreamed of. "What hath God wrought" was the message that Samuel F.B. Morse tapped in 1844 to officially open the first telegraph line from Washington to Baltimore. Little did he know. Technology advances at a dizzying pace, and though I'm not the one developing it, I'm certainly implementing it and finding ways to use it effectively.

CHAPTER FOUR

The
Human
Touch

You probably remember *Cheers*, that long-running television show from the '80s set in a Boston bar where the customers and employees were like family. "Where Everybody Knows Your Name" was the refrain from the show's theme song. You may even know a neighborhood stop like that: "That's where my friends will be," you tell yourself, "so that's where I'll go hang out."

"Relationship selling" is today's buzzword, though it's hardly a new concept: Smart retailers long have known that a customer who feels among friends will keep coming back. Other businesses still have that "ice cubes and the Eskimo" mentality: They don't understand the value of the one-on-one, personal approach, service with a handshake.

With an effective on-hold network, your company can help callers feel as if they're part of the family. The idea isn't to hit them with a sales barrage; instead, you want to help them get to know you. You want to tell them what your company is all about. You want to use that on-hold time to say so much more than "thanks for holding." Yet that's all that some businesses think they need when they come to us.

> With an effective on-hold network, your company can help callers feel as if they're part of the family. A customer who feels among friends will keep coming back.

The voice-over acting for your on-hold production should sound natural and friendly and reflect the culture of your company. At Phone On-Hold®, we have a variety of voice-over actors from which you can choose, and we learn everything we can about your company culture. This is an opportunity to bond with your caller. You could mention the little league team you sponsor, or your support for the Rotary Foundation, or the fact that your longtime receptionist just had a baby.

You've no doubt heard the same approach on TV news programs when the anchor slips in a comment about some member of the staff you never see: "Lisa's going on maternity leave. We're going to miss her." Networks know the personal approach attracts viewers. Business should know it attracts and keeps customers and clients.

It Works For Us

It's the approach we use when we're dealing with our own prospects. We want, of course, to get the agreement. We want them to buy our services—or, to put it another way, we want to be of service to them.

And that's the key. We believe that developing a good relationship will make the sales happen for our own benefit and for theirs.

Relationship selling is an approach that works for us. Then, once a business is using the on-hold service we provide, it in effect will be using that same approach to attract customers of its own. We want our clients to make use of our talent and creative ability to develop the relationships that will grow business.

It comes down to this: You need to love people—and that involves respecting them, valuing them, sharing with them, and wanting to be with them, to talk to them. That's what builds relationships, and that's what gets you the sale. Whether you are selling door to door, in a shop, or online, you are dealing with the fundamental human need to communicate. It's our nature.

Communicating well is so important that companies should train employees on how to do it, just in case a less pleasant aspect of their nature should arise under workaday pressures. It's good to get to know people. In the old days, doctors visited the family on house calls. Townsfolk joked with the shopkeeper. That's how relationships were built. Times are changing, sure—but we need to hold on to the tenets of what makes people tick. We are made to communicate.

The lesson: Take time with your customers and treat them well. Make them feel they matter. Once you make that human connection, you can better assess their needs because they'll be more open to telling you. And when you know their needs, you have learned what you can sell them to serve them best.

A good salesman doesn't talk a prospect into anything. A good salesman just tells the honest truth, and if there's a fit, great. If not, that should be fine too. Technically, a salesman is a consultant—a sales consultant. Even if you're in the business of selling ice cubes, you shouldn't want to see an Eskimo buying them.

> **If you take time with your customers and make them feel they matter, they'll be more open to telling you their needs. And when you know their needs, you know what to sell them that will serve them best.**

If you truly enjoy people and are empathetic, you'll fare far better in the marketplace. I know this to be true from my own success in sales and from my relationships in community organizations such as Chambers of Commerce and Rotary International. If you like people, it's even fun to make cold calls. A lot of salesmen hate cold calls, but I see them as a great opportunity to meet people. If you go right for the sales pitch, you sound like every other cold call the prospect receives. How do you know whether what you have to offer will work for the prospect before you collect any information? I start with a light-hearted approach and then ask for advice. And indeed I do need advice—I want to make sure I'm talking to the correct contact in the company. "I'm just hoping the right person could take a look at what we do and see if there is a glove fit between our companies, " I say, and no longer am I perceived as some pushy salesman. And in truth I am not.

People are interested in solutions, and you can appeal to them by presenting yourself as a solver instead of as a seller. Show that you're truly interested in them and that you're primarily interested in helping and informing, not in cashing in. This is the winning attitude to adopt with your business prospects: "I want to find a solution for you, and if I don't have it myself I'll find somebody for you who does."

It's the approach I take when I have to deal with the occasional irate caller. "I'm here to solve this for you," I say, "so let's figure it out." By working diligently on a problem, real or perceived, you can turn that angry caller into a loyal customer. Emphasize service. Go above and beyond. I drive a Volvo, and a service underwriter at a Volvo dealership named Bill Bruno made me want to return again and again. He always remembered my name, for one. Once, he pointed out that a lightbulb had come loose on my car and took a moment to plug it back in for me. Small gestures like that build relationships.

Engage Your Callers

The same holds true with your on-hold network. Engage your callers. You can still create a message that delivers a strong product sell—after all, one can't disregard the need to make a profit and get a return on investment—but remember your network is primarily a non-sales environment in the mind of your caller. The emphasis must be on relationship, engaging the caller and cultivating a positive customer experience, and a properly designed on-hold network will accomplish that.

But it is the wrong medium to make an overt sales pitch, such as you might create with jingles and radio commercials. It's a common mistake to use such methods—"We've got great deals, c'mon down, half price today only!"—in an on-hold network. It's a different channel and must be addressed as such. Instead, offer useful consumer tips, help them get to know your employees, and invite them to ask for details about the great sale when they come in. Engage, inform—and the sales will follow.

The on-hold experience can actually be more productive than the customer service. This is what happened recently when I called a business:

"Thanks for calling," a woman said, hastily. "Be with you in a minute; could you please hold?" Click. I heard nothing until a minute later, when she suddenly came back on the line.

"What do you want?" she said.

"Excuse me?"

"Oh, I'm sorry," she said. "I picked up the wrong line. Can I help you?"

"Uh, I'd like to speak with Mr. Smith, please."

"Who are you?"

"Pete Turpel."

"What do you want?"

At that point I wasn't sure if I still wanted anything. I felt embarrassed for her and the poor perception of her company that she was communicating to callers. Businesses should treat callers like royalty, yet too often they act as if the customer is there for them instead of vice versa.

Customers, too, can sometimes be very difficult, perhaps because they're so accustomed to poor treatment. But staffs do get very busy, and wait time is inevitable; it's unreasonable for callers to think they'll never be placed on hold. The staff can feel mistreated, and they're dealing with their own frustrations. Still, they must be trained to deal effectively with all types. You can't mistreat a customer, because the "Rule of 200" comes into play: Do something nice for me, I'll tell one person. Do something bad, I'll tell 200. That's the way your reputation spreads. It's sort of like compounding interest. It happens one increment at a time, but it builds and it builds.

> **You can't mistreat a customer, because the "Rule of 200" comes into play: Do something nice for me, I'll tell one person. Do something bad, I'll tell 200. That's the way your reputation spreads.**

You can't please everybody. There's just no way. A customer who is waiting can become tense and angry—particularly in call centers and on customer service lines, where the customer may be calling with a complaint and may feel irritated for having to contact you in the first place. Dealing with that is one reason an effective on-hold network is so important. It can get the caller's mind off the wait with entertainment and information. If you don't do that right, all you're going to do is raise the frustration level. The person may already be feeling ill-used, so he's not in the mood to hear how much you appreciate his business—and, once again, you don't want to thank him for holding. He's annoyed that he's holding in the first place.

Everything is about expectations. People want respect when they are taking the time to patronize a company. Who wouldn't? Instead of frustrating your callers by giving them the silent treatment or playing music, you have the opportunity to educate and inform. You can let callers know they are valuable and important to you. Building the relationship builds loyalty and pays dividends.

That's particularly important in this age of rapid-fire communication, with technology changing so fast that customers aren't sure when to adopt it. Consider what a great feat it must have been to sell the first fax machine. How do you persuade someone to buy a machine that nobody else has? The sale must have been based on the potential—and that's the educational role that a good salesperson should fill. In today's Internet culture, the fax machine seems almost like a dinosaur. Communication and information come in a twinkling; one might think it old-fashioned, almost inefficient, to listen to a voice.

But the Web has its limits. As a matter of fact, recent holiday season statistics showed that Web sales actually went down. As companies such as Google and eBay conduct business in a much broader way, it's easy to forget the primacy of the personal relationship. Even if your business is set up to serve customers on the Internet, you still have to communicate that personal relationship to them. You can't build a business relationship as easy on the Internet as compared to the magic of the telephone and the human voice.

People long for the human touch. The human voice remains the fundamental communication. Most employers—in the United States, more than 80 percent—are small businesses. People still walk in the door. Technology doesn't trump relationships. The handshake will never be antiquated.

CHAPTER FIVE

Evolving Technology

Mabel the secretary knew something had to be done: The callers kept hanging up in frustration. "I need some way to page you," she told her boss, Mr. Johnson, a car dealer. "You're always out on the lot with customers, and I have no way to reach you."

So their technicians worked some magic, and now Mabel had a speaker system ("Mr. Johnson, call on line two"). Then someone suggested that those speakers might as well play music for customers as they look at cars, and the technicians jumped to the task—they even piped the radio station out there.

Mabel was still unhappy. "The trouble is people still hang up after a minute or so," she told Mr. Johnson. "They think we've hung up on them." So the sound guys plugged in a computer card so that callers on hold also could hear the radio station—copyright law notwithstanding.

That's when companies such as Phone On-Hold® came along. We told them about the legal risks involved in rebroadcasting radio and let them know we had a much more effective tool to engage their callers. And that, in essence, is how the on-hold network industry started in the early 1980s.

I first grasped the potential on that day back in 1984 when my friend asked me to plug the radio station into his telephone system. Instead, I wondered, wouldn't he be better served by playing some sort of production for callers that talked about his pool supply business?

Even when I took my business full time nearly a decade later, not many companies were doing that. But the industry was growing, particularly in Florida. A company called Original Message On Hold was trying to franchise the concept across the country.

The Early Days

An entrepreneur named Rick Hodges of Audio Marketing Systems, Inc. (dba: AMS Messages-On-Hold) in Culver City, California, had introduced what may have been the first On-Hold Network back in 1980, for a Los Angeles company. That was before the era of digital equipment. When I started, I used cassette recorders. Hodges used a device called a cart machine, which played "carts" that looked like thin eight-track tapes. The primary provider was Fidelipac. Broadcasters recorded commercials onto carts, and the machine would reset them to the beginning for the next use. Hodges found that it also worked well for his On-Hold Network.

Also in the early days, Telephonetics cut a deal with AT&T in which practically every phone system that AT&T sold had a Telephonetics player. AT&T eventually bought the company and renamed the service Magic On Hold. The content was consistent with the norm of the day—simply general information, "thanks for holding" announcements, and other platitudes and apologetics. That was the prevailing style, and frankly I did the same thing in the beginning. "We're sorry you're on hold. We appreciate your business." A lot of providers still take that approach, even as more and more clients recognize the potential for so much more.

The technology was evolving rapidly, and along came the age of digital players.

The technology was evolving rapidly, and along came the age of digital players and their manufacturers. First, they came out with systems that let you plug a cassette machine into a digital player and record the content. That was a big step up from endless-loop cassette as audio tape eventually disintegrates. But the new technology let us transfer the audio to a digital chip. No moving parts and nothing to wear out. But still you had to listen to each production, three minutes long for each location. Can you imagine if you had three hundred of those?

Then the manufacturer Bogen introduced an inexpensive automatic digital download. With this machine, you could put in a cassette tape and the audio content would download automatically onto a digital chip. The audio would then play off the digital chip, eliminating the problem of moving parts that could wear out.

Other manufacturers were Nel-Tech; Mackenzie Laboratories; and Premier Technologies, which came out with a well-built machine called the ADL (automatic download). I'd been considering the Bogen system, but Premier salesman Todd Griffin told me his company's system was under development but he could send me what he had so far. It would work pretty well, he said. What he sent me was a digital player with a Sony Walkman double-sticky-taped on top of it with a little audio cord connecting the two together. "You've got to be kidding me!" I said. But we became good friends. He later started his own company called Solutions On Hold, and it was Griffin who informed me of the Florida meeting that was the genesis of OHMA (On Hold Messaging Association).

Breakthroughs

The remote-load systems made life far easier in the on-hold world. Previously, it had worked like this: If a client had three hundred locations nationwide, I made three hundred tapes and sent them out. Then the company might decide to run a promotion and ask me to change the script. I would have to create another audio production and send out three hundred more cassettes by snail mail. It wasn't efficient, but it was all we had.

With a remote-load unit, the client could connect the device to a telephone line, and if anybody wanted a change, I could deliver it in a day. The problem, though, was that too often when I tried to call the unit to make the changes, somebody would answer the phone or an answering machine would interrupt the call. So the next evolution was an RUF, remote upload fax. It connected to a fax line, which only the fax machine uses. The RUF would answer, and if it was me calling it would record my changes to the script; otherwise, the RUF passed the call through to the fax.

Technology was changing at a maddeningly fast pace, as it still is today. DSL came out, and companies began using it on their fax lines. Our RUF players conflicted with the DSL on the fax line, so we had to install filters. Another issue we faced was the technology was analog, which meant we uploaded the audio production in real time. If the production was six minutes long, and I had to download it to three hundred units, you can imagine the hours involved.

Premier Technologies, the manufacturer we chose to use, then came out with the DDF, which stands for digital download and fax. The digital box used a software program and talked modem to modem, communicating with ones and zeros. We'd create the audio production, run it through the software, and dial out to the location to transfer the production digitally.

With software, we could do the mixing in the box. Imagine a bookcase with ninety-nine shelves. The top shelf is where you put your music, and on the other shelves you put individual messages. The box would play the music, lower the volume to play one of the messages on the other shelves, and then bring the music back up. And you had a playlist so you could play message one, message ten, message eleven, message fourteen, message fifteen. Suppose one message said, "We'll be at the trade show; come see us at Booth 2574." When that trade show was over, we could pull out that one message without changing the whole production—a lot more versatility, and far faster.

That was in the late 1990s, and technology has continued to speed up. Along came Voice-Over Internet Protocol, or VoIP—telephone systems such as Cisco, ShoreTel and others that don't use traditional lines but, rather, the Internet.

When we tried to sell on-hold networks, potential clients would tell us they didn't need us because their technicians had advised them that the phone system was able to do what we do. So now we're back to educating: "Is your phone system," we say, "actually going to create an audio production for you to use? Or is it just going to play it for you?" It's the same old struggle. They think they just need music, and they miss a terrific communication and marketing opportunity.

Music, however, requires Internet bandwidth to play, and the VoIP developers didn't want to borrow bandwidth needed for voice—the quality of conversations was bad enough, with voices often breaking up or blocking each other. So the engineers allowed little bandwidth for the music or the message; we had to compress it down so far that it sounded dreadful. That situation has improved: With most of the VoIP systems coming out today, we can hook up an external player to manage the content for clients without having to get IT involved. The quality of sound remains good when people are placed on hold or transferred.

More recent developments include a delivery system for audio files over the Internet. The unit connects to the company's LAN network and communicates with our servers, checking for any updates. If it finds an updated audio file, it uploads it and begins delivering the information to the business callers. That development has made installation of an on-hold network extremely simple. It helps us to focus our energies on the many details of what really matters for our clients: a unique and professional on-hold communication tool.

Communication Is Still the Key

The technology has indeed come a long way, and it was the talent and hard work of the engineers and IT professionals that made it happen. Now it's time to put that technology to use in the most effective way to advance your business.

What you should be getting in a good on-hold network is an effective communication channel that markets your business as you wish to portray it, complementing what you do with radio, TV, direct mail, or print. In making the best use of such a network, it's time for the IT department to step aside and for the marketing department to do what it does best. You don't consult with your IT or phone technicians when designing brochures or ads, so why get them involved with your on-hold network?

Those engineers did bring us remarkable abilities. For example, at Phone On-Hold® we now can update our services with national sports and entertainment news daily. We are the first on-hold provider in the country to do so. Clients might ask why we'd want to do that, since sports and entertainment might have nothing to do with their particular business. The reason is this: It helps them sound different from everybody else...and engage the caller.

The talent and hard work of engineers and IT professionals gave us amazing technology. But you don't consult with them when designing brochures or ads, so why get them involved with your on-hold network?

Callers expect to just hear, "Thanks for holding. We'll be with you in a moment," and maybe a few words about all the cool stuff the company does. The caller's perception is just like every other disappointing experience they have ever had while waiting. Instead, with our audio content, they have an entirely different attitude about the company and the time they are waiting. We can even place daily national, sports and entertainment news on our client's on-hold network. Why? Because we want our clients to sound different from the rest and we want their callers to have a positive perception of the time they are spending with the company.

It's another way of engaging the caller. All those engineering advances are wasted if that isn't paramount. The technology could evolve into telepathy, for that matter, and it would profit a company little if its callers still were left feeling mistreated. The callers will blame you for the failings of your telecommunication network. And if they do, then you should blame your service provider. At Phone On-Hold®, we strive constantly to get it right, presenting the latest creative breakthroughs to our clients in a way that keeps their own customers coming back with a positive perception and customer experience with the company.

CHAPTER SIX

The Misleading Allure of VoIP

"That's a pretty cool invention you've got there, Mr. Bell, but all those wires! You should check out VoIP."

"Pardon?"

"Voice Over Internet Protocol. It makes your invention there seem like tin cans and string. With VoIP, all the telephone calls go out over your Internet connection, and there's no charge. Everybody's talking about it. Vonage. Cisco. ShoreTel. Allworx."

"Inter-what?"

"Net. It uses the Internet. What a concept! What a savings! Now a company can have an On-Hold Network and just pay for one digital player serving a hundred locations."

"On-Hold Network? What's that do?"

Forgive my flight of fancy there, but at least Alexander Graham Bell's ignorance would be understandable, given his nineteenth-century technological handicap. It's less understandable why today's business owners would fall for the misleading allure of VoIP for delivery of their on-hold network. Yet many do. Like Bell, they really don't know what an On-Hold Network can do.

With VoIP, on-hold service providers face the same challenge that has arisen at every step of the technological ladder: getting clients to understand that what we do is all about marketing, image and branding. Anyone can slap a recording onto a distribution device. But what does it say? How is it developed? Does it deliver the image the company wants to project? Does it engage the caller, or enrage?

Those are the same questions we've asked all along. It's a point so important that this book emphasizes it in every chapter: Companies need to see the potential for a powerful communications tool. No matter what technological marvels await us, they'll never replace the importance of building relationships and marketing savvy.

Business owners may feel VoIP can get them more for their dollar because, wow, they only need one little unit and one audio file and they'll reach dozens of their locations. That's what their IT personnel whisper in their ears. The trouble is, the company then has to manage that file's contents and any changes it wants to make to it. And each of those many locations is different: A VoIP system used with one audio file homogenizes them and sacrifices flexibility. In a national chain of stores, for example, the on-hold network should be able to adjust for local variations in demo and psychographics as well as simple things like operating hours and directions, or on promotions and specials offered. The voice should reflect the local accent and dialect. Store policies likely will differ.

> A company may feel VoIP gets it more for its dollar because, wow, one little unit and one audio file reaches dozens of locations. The trouble is, the company has to manage that file and any changes. And each location is very different.

Don't get me wrong: VoIP is good. It's an exciting development. But any VoIP system that a company considers should allow flexibility. Most every VoIP system still does have an input for an external player so that the on-hold provider can manage the client's network, delivering and revising and tailoring the content. The company should use that input. A good role for the IT department is to install the system—and then its job should be done.

Let's look at the technological specifics: One limitation is the playing of the on-hold production in "Unicast," meaning the recording starts anew whenever a call goes on hold. Since the average on-hold time is half a minute, the caller hears the same opening each time, and that's a small portion of what's available on a production lasting several minutes. "Multicast" allows the production to loop, but most VoIP systems default to Unicast.

"ACD" or Automatic Call Distribution plays a music stream interrupted by announcements—an annoying practice that was the brainchild of an engineer. It's also older technology, yet IT staff may recommend it, thinking it saves the company money. What it does instead is rob the company of its image and the opportunities inherent in an on-hold network.

A VoIP system uses Internet bandwidth, a limited resource for any company. A streamed audio file can degrade the quality of voice transmissions in a telephone conversation, and it can hinder data transfer. Even if the IT staff allocates bandwidth properly, the extra load on the bandwidth can still cause problems—the audio file may need to be compressed, wreaking havoc on sound quality. But the IT staff may not be inclined to give the issue much priority. Or the staff may be outsourced, making it harder for the business to resolve problems at hand. In either case, the IT staff would be unlikely to pay much attention to loading timely updates for the diverse locations, particularly since that content would further strain bandwidth.

The lesson for on-hold clients is this: You get what you pay for. Our rate is based on the level of creativity and our company resources that you choose to use, and clients can change the production as they wish. We provide the talent, the creative consultants, the music and studio time, and the fulfillment and support staff. The result: a versatile marketing tool tailored to your business. Before you buy a VoIP system, consider how it will affect your branding ability: The IT or phone system salesperson doesn't really care about the image of your company.

> **You get what you pay for. We provide a versatile marketing tool tailored to your business. Before a company buys a VoIP system, it should consider how it will affect branding ability.**

If you operate a large company and are launching a major advertising campaign, you need to be sensitive to the demographics and psychographics of your target market. You don't want to run the same advertisements in, say, Pontiac, Michigan, as you do in Los Angeles. Let me emphasize again: A VoIP system should allow that flexibility, and some do not—though the providers and manufacturers increasingly have recognized the merit.

An on-hold network is designed to take the project off the client's desk. We manage the whole affair—producing it, managing the audio files, taking care of any changes—and the company reaps the benefits. If a company opts to have its IT department manage those files, it adds another layer of service. The IT staff is dealing with other daily concerns—"Fix my computer!" and "What's wrong with my phone?"—so the new duty of managing those time-sensitive on-hold files is going to fall way to the bottom of its priorities. Having an On-Hold Network becomes a burden for the company instead of a breeze.

There's no reason that VoIP should pose a challenge to the on-hold industry. Though it might seem to offer do-it-yourself capabilities to businesses, most of them are not prepared, lack the resources and time, and do not want to do it themselves. Once they understand the importance of what we do, they recognize our continuing role as a communications channel they can't afford to lose.

CHAPTER SEVEN

Voices of the Past

S ailing is the essence of simplicity. Whisked along by the wind, you feel at one with the ocean, as sailors have felt since they first ventured out to sea—which is to say, since the dawn of human history. When I'm out in my 30-foot sailboat, I feel something ancient, a sense of adventure, and I feel in tune with the elements and the elemental. The ocean must be where God lives.

Modern sailboats have what is known as a main furler in the mast. It's quite a handy invention and can save a lot of fuss, and that's all very nice. But I still raise, lower and fold the main sail myself. That way I know that if I ever have to get it down manually, I can do it. And I like the look. I like to see that sail draped over the boom. It looks like a sailboat.

I've been sailing virtually my entire life. I accompanied my father, starting when I was six and he was stationed with the Navy out of Pearl Harbor. Would I find a sunken ship? Maybe I could find a trove of treasures. I was a boy enthralled by the sense of adventure.

And today I'm a man enthralled by the sense of adventure. I've been in Rotary for twenty-three years, and sometimes at meetings we have an exercise called "Craft Talks" in which we pose questions for discussion. One question recently was this: "If you could do anything and do it for free, what would you do?" The first thing that popped into my mind was to be a treasure hunter. I think of the diver who found the Antioch, the wreckage of a Spanish galleon in Bermuda, and the thrill of picking up those coins. Or those first images sent from the ocean floor upon the discovery of the Titanic: I was intrigued to see a shoe, a dining plate—the stuff of daily human doings, so long undersea.

The Spirit of Discovery

The allure of diving shipwrecks involves far more than finding riches. It's the spirit of discovery. The inventors who were the vanguard of our technological revolution likewise embraced that spirit. In our whirlpool of technology we may ask, as did that early telegraph message, what God has wrought—though I still can't help but to think God prefers the slow and timeless surge of the ocean's currents, or the wide and eternal swing of the Earth around the sun. Those are the timepieces of history, keeping perfect cadence no matter how hectic life gets upon our globe.

Technology does fascinate me. My business could not exist without it. But mostly I'm in the business of people, and communicating—and therefore I'm fascinated, too, by the lives of our forebears who brought us so many marvelous inventions, a testament to man's yearning to learn. I want to hear the voices of the past.

Go to a museum, and experience the wonderment of antiquities. All things historical intrigue me, too: people, their possessions, how they lived. It's the feeling of glimpsing the past anew that you get upon returning to the family home after many years away and encountering your childhood: your old baseball bat tucked in a closet, the yard where once you played. In my office, I still have the stereo console with turntable that my dad gave my mom for an anniversary present back in '66. It still works. I still have my grandfather's old Zippo lighter, a hundred years old. I hold it and can feel the past.

Technology fascinates me. My business could not exist without it. But mostly I'm in the business of people, and communicating. All things historical intrigue me, too: people, their possessions, how they lived.

That's why I collect old telephones and equipment. I have an array of devices, many of them working, in my home and office, and I've even had my eye on a 1938 oaken telephone booth that a man I know might be willing to sell. He has it in his garage: It came from an old building in Los Angeles and was destined for the landfill, and he asked if he could have it. It still has the old pay phone inside. I'd like to put it my office and see if I can get it to work.

I have some vintage advertisements, and they, too, reveal how we once were. Telephones come in many styles, and I often wonder what the designers were thinking. Why did they want it shaped like this? Why did they put it like that? I wonder about those who made them and those who used them. Some were designed strictly for function; others were designed for lifestyle. Popular among the wealthy in the 1970s was the elegantly boxed phone. And teenagers of the time liked the "donut" phone, with its mod circular design.

The old ads tell a story of our changing culture and values. A 1930s ad for the American Telephone and Telegraph Company (AT&T) in the *Literary Digest* that proclaims, in big letters, "He is calling you." True to the times, the ad was male-centric. Another advertisement tells of men around the world who contributed to the phone: A Japanese man who prepared the silk for the cord, a "swarthy miner" of mica in British India, an Irishman who raised flax used in the condenser, a Brazilian who drained rubber from a tree for use in the receiver. And then the ad brings it back to America: "He is one of 28,000 men and women at Western Electric that work in Chicago. From a slab of rubber, a bundle of vegetable and animal fibers, and a curious medley of minerals brought from every corner of the world, this man's skill produces a marvel of precision and ruggedness: your telephone."

That ad rings out with pride, and it reminds us even today of the importance of people—how the toil of people around the world is what brings it all together to produce this "marvel" that gives us the ability to communicate from many thousands of miles away. It's a tribute to those who made the telephone and those who designed it for new and better uses.

I like to think I'm among today's designers—not of the physical style of the phone, but in the way it is used as a communication channel. Technology has accelerated our world, and people today become impatient if they feel their time is being wasted. An on-hold network keeps them engaged in a busy world.

If Those Walls Could Only Talk

My interest in history is related to my hobby of ghost hunting. It's a natural interest for one who is enamored of people, history, and communication: Is it possible to feel the presence of those who lived before us? People ask me whether I believe in ghosts. "I believe in God," I tell them: The paranormal is not a religion to me, but I enjoy the study of it. I go on ghost hunts not because I want or expect to see a ghost—in fact, our purpose is to debunk—but because I like going to where they're supposed to be. It's a way of experiencing the places, the history.

I recently joined a group on a tour of the Holly Mont Castles, reputed to be most haunted houses in Hollywood. The actress Barbara Stanwyck once lived there. A tunnel that may have been used during the Prohibition era connects the basements of the houses, which are mirror images of each other. As the story goes, the owner of one of the houses once found a tombstone of a young woman named Regina in the tunnel. He sealed the tunnel on his end. The owner of the other house, the one we toured, says he has kept the basement doors locked for the ten years he's lived there because it's just too creepy down there.

The ghost of Regina, he told us, haunts his house; once in a while, he says, he'll find the dining room table chandelier's light bulbs removed and laid out on the table. He agreed to try to open the basement door for our group, which was the first to investigate hauntings there in many years. But the knob just turned without engaging, as it did for several of us who tried to open the door. When I tried, I said, "Come on, Regina, help me out here," and the door opened right up. It was chilling, and fun. And when we went down into the basement, we found a stash of pictures—old photographs of people who had resided there.

I've never seen a ghost. Once, however, I was staying at one of the shotgun houses that my sister Kathleen buys and fixes up in New

Orleans, and I couldn't sleep: I kept hearing footsteps, and looking out the window I thought I saw a man in a puffy white shirt cross the yard and walk out the back wall. The house is near the canal in the area where pirates once frequented, but in New Orleans I imagine pirates were everywhere. Another time, a kindergarten teacher told us she would put the classroom toys away each afternoon, only to find them stacked in the middle of the room in the morning. As we investigated, I felt a brush against my leg. But I told the group that I believed it was my imagination. One must remain very skeptical because your "experience" may only be wishful thinking. We investigated that kindergarten room, and even installed cameras, but didn't pick up anything. Yet it was so interesting. It was an adventure.

One must respect the past, I believe, and learn about it, and preserve it—and thus my office collection of dozens of antique phones. I even have what I call the first portable phone—two cans with a string. I use it as a humorous illustration during speaking engagements. So much has changed even in the last generation or two that our children are baffled at how we lived. At home I have an old Western Electric 554 wall phone, the type popular in the late '60s and early '70s. When we first got it, I'd point to it when my children's friends would ask to call home. "There's the phone right there," I'd say, and they'd just stare at it.

> One must respect the past, I believe, and learn about it, and preserve it—and thus my office collection of dozens of antique phones.

A friend was telling me that his wife, who likes antiques, plugged in a 1940s rotary desktop phone in their house. Their 9-year-old daughter tried to use it and reported to her that it was broken. "What's wrong?" his wife asked their daughter. "It was working fine." It seems she was trying to press the numbers instead of dialing.

"Everything is amazing and nobody's happy," comedian Louis C.K. told late-night host Conan O'Brien. It seems he was on an airplane that temporarily lost the connection on its new Wi-Fi feature, and a young passenger next to him was furious for the inconvenience, though he'd only just learned about it five minutes before. New wonders seem to just add to some people's frustrations. Once, the biggest inconvenience was having to wait while dialing the phone because a number had too many zeros.

One might think I'd have little patience with antiques, considering that I'm a man who keeps abreast of technology and how it can best serve my clients. But it is quite the opposite: I love the feeling of connection that antiques give us with the past. I'm fascinated by what might lie hidden within the walls of old houses. The possibility of finding old letters during a renovation intrigues me; like those vintage advertisements, they would be a glimpse into the past. That's why I enjoy the HGTV show *If Walls Could Talk*—the things they find in old houses reveal so much about those who owned and used them. It's a concept that engages people's hearts.

Slowing Down, Keeping It Real

We must keep technology in perspective. Nobody's happy with our amazing advances because we're moving so quickly. Technology can not only enhance our experiences but it also can tear us apart by preventing us from sitting down and thinking. In our advances, and in our rush to get somewhere, we do lose something, but we can hold on to the best.

That's why I prefer taking the surface streets to work rather than the freeway. You travel slower and see more of what is around you. Have you ever wanted to say hello to a friend and he's poking at his Blackberry and hardly notices any of his surroundings? Go into any meeting today, and watch everybody pull out their little devices and start checking text messages. I think what we're really tearing ourselves apart from is our inner selves. We don't get in touch with what we think anymore.

Once, everything had to be written down on paper, which I think is why people had such a greater command of the English language than we do today. I can't stand the way people spell when they text. "You are" becomes "U R." People used to write with flair and elegance. Take a look at some of the letters written by Civil War soldiers, without education, and note the elaborate writing and strong penmanship.

Technology is supposed to save us time, but sometimes it just makes us do more, unnecessarily. It's like the guy who's speeding down the freeway at 80 miles an hour: I may be behind him going the speed limit, and he's going to get there only two or three minutes ahead of me. Or the guy who beeps to pass you—and then he gets to a stoplight and you pull up alongside him, nice and slow.

I'm guilty, too, of trying to cram too much into a day, but some things must not be missed, no matter how pressing your obligations. I set other things aside for my son's ballgame, for example. And recently I gave an elderly gentleman a ride home because he'd gone to the corner store and was too worn out to walk back. It comes down to the human experience: We need to help people and love them. We must not get too busy living that we forget to live.

> **Technology is supposed to save us time, but sometimes it just makes us do more—and we must not get too busy living that we forget to live.**

Because we don't pause to consider where we're going, I think we miss a lot of opportunities. From my perspective, I believe that businesses, too, lose that opportunity for human contact when they don't pay attention to how their telephone systems are being operated and how their customers on hold are being treated. They have an opportunity to engage the caller. You can build customers forever that way. It's an example of how technology can serve us and humanize us in this all-too-often impersonal world.

Used properly, technology can free us. One of the greatest freedoms I've known is the feeling while skydiving. Today's technology has added greatly to the art of skydiving—can you imagine those who jumped from a plane for the first time and the basic equipment they were dealing with? We can thank technology for making the experience safer and more relaxing and allowing a greater sense of freedom.

I admire the pioneers of flight. Visit the National Air and Space Museum in Washington, and you'll marvel at the accomplishments, and the sheer daring. Think of the Wright brothers: "Let's build this contraption," they more or less said, "and climb aboard and see if it works." For those pioneers, the pursuit of freedom through the advance of technology was a matter of life and death. The spirit of adventure, and discovery, propelled them.

For better and for worse, it's a different world—and a far less simple one. The younger generations will never experience that sense of childhood freedom that many of us knew. Remember when mom and dad would just call out or whistle from the front porch that it was time to come home for dinner? Now the kids get a cell phone call or a text message. More and more people don't even get land lines anymore, and if we have a major disaster the cellular networks will be the first to go out. That infrastructure is so tenuous.

But even though young people may mock those primitive rotary phones we used, and even though we all marvel at the latest technological potentials, let's remind one another of the basics: Whether we use tin cans or the Internet, what's important is effective communication. The bottom line is that one person must connect to another person in a way that makes it real. It's as simple as that.

CHAPTER EIGHT

As Good As It Gets

I n traditional advertising, salesmen look for tens of thousands of dollars a year from a client. The average rate a business pays for an on-hold network is only $1,000 a year. That's about $90 a month. If you were to tell me that your advertising budget was $90 a month, I couldn't imagine what sort of ads you'd be buying. You might be able to get on the back of your church bulletin, but that's about it.

Yet not everyone whom an advertisement reaches will be motivated to buy. A certain amount of the ad purchaser's money is in a sense thrown away. By contrast, when you have people on your telephone line, you've already gotten the phone to ring. You know they're interested in you. And that's what makes an on-hold network a far more targeted, effective communication channel.

> An on-hold network's return on invest-
> ment is huge. When you build a relation-
> ship with customers, you cultivate their
> loyalty.

An effective system increases employee efficiency. It can help to relieve the staff of annoyances that can come up in dealing with people and remove some of the burdens that can fray tempers. But it's also quite a time saver. Many businesses get countless phone calls from people who merely want to know hours of operation and directions. That information can be delivered while the caller is on hold. The customer's time has been used well. The staff's time has been used well. Productivity and satisfaction both rise.

For $90 a month, the return on investment is huge. When you build a relationship with customers, you cultivate their loyalty. Eighty percent of a company's profits comes from twenty percent of its customers, as the adage goes, so the benefit to the bottom line can be profound—that is, if the on-hold network is created properly.

What Our Clients Say

At Phone On-Hold® Marketing, we make sure we're doing it right by consulting regularly with our clients. Every six months, we send out a customer survey and ask them how we're doing. We pay the most attention to any comments that lean toward the negative—and I'm pleased to say that's only about one or two percent. We want to discover any problems and concerns and address them. You can't always please everybody, but we want to come as close as we can.

One question we ask is: "What is your favorite feature regarding your On-Hold Network service?" Here's one response to that: "I love the newsletters." We send out a monthly newsletter to our clients as yet one more way to enhance communications. It's not about selling anything—rather, we offer tips on business and employee relations, and fun features, such as a drink of the month named after one of the employees.

Here's another response to that question: "It's very easy to change and work with you guys; we can listen to the background music online, and changing the script is very easy. Quick response, great customer service." And another: "Good tech support, good voice talent and creative, ease of process—we select the type of music and submit. The ability to update as often as our marketing needs dictate." And here's a client who says, "Customer service is excellent and fast turnaround."

To the question, "What would you like to see change regarding your on-hold networking service?," one client responded: "Nothing. I think the service is great. Can't think of anything." That's the kind of feedback that lets us know we're on the right track.

But to be perfectly candid, we need to look for places where we might not be doing so well. We look for any voids in our service and strive to fill them. That is what any on-hold provider should be doing, and so many of them don't. Sometimes it's a matter of getting the word out more effectively about what we offer. One client suggested we should have a wider range of licensed music. We do have thousands of choices available, but obviously we needed to communicate that better. We emphasized those choices again on our website, created links for online searches, and added information about music selection to the on-hold network. Communication, once again, was the key.

> We look for any voids in our service and strive to fill them. That is what any on-hold provider should be doing, and so many of them don't.

"I'm very happy with the service," a client responded when asked to comment on how Phone On-Hold® Marketing's services compared with other providers. "You take care of me, and then I do not have to take care of you. That's the best part."

What pleases that client is that he doesn't have to constantly police us. There's no need to prod us along—"Is the production done? Where is it? Does it include what we asked? Have you sent it?" That client is experiencing salesmanship and service as it is meant to be. We have a solution, and we competently provide an array of services that the client truly can use.

Our Services

Creating the content for a company's on-hold network makes up about 90 percent of Phone On-Hold® Marketing System's business. But we also provide in-store music, in-store broadcasting services, professionally recorded voice mail to e-mail services, other call-handling solutions and advanced digital signage services that we call ASIRA Business Vision. Companies such as mine should work to enhance the entire scope of a company's branding, and that includes the customer experience whether on the phone or in the store. Following are some of the services we offer to our appreciative clients.

Call Handler Solution

This service is particularly useful for phone orders and was designed with the fast-food industry in mind, though it can be used in many ways: When a customer calls, the system answers the phone and delivers what we call an upsell. Then the call rings through to the staff; if the staff has to ask the customer to wait again, the system delivers a different piece of audio content. It has a 24/7 clock in it, so the customer might hear, for example: "Hey, it's Monday night football tonight, so don't forget an extra order of chicken wings." The system knows whether to say "good morning," "good afternoon," or "good evening," or whether to advise that the office is closed and when it reopens.

The Call Handler Solution's return on investment is phenomenal. It delivers that upsell right when the caller is thinking about what to order, and the suggestion is short and immediate. The caller is inclined to add the suggested purchase to the order, increasing the average phone order sales ticket.

Another advantage of the Call Handler Solution is its ability to deal with diversity. We're a country of many ethnicities and dialects and regional accents. It can be hard enough to understand what people are saying, and sometimes they talk so fast. Callers can get frustrated, but this system provides a clear and concise message, maintains the company's branding, and is perfect every single time. One company with six locations in the San Fernando Valley finds that our system helps in its frequent dealings with the Hispanic population. The company does have Hispanics on staff, but it also has Persians and mumbling Americans, and the Call Handler makes sure the phone is consistently answered the same, perfect way each and every time. The company's image and brand is intact with every call.

We deal with regional dialects all around the country and also throughout Canada. The French spoken in Ontario is not the same as in France. If we're doing Spanish in Puerto Rico, it will be different than the Spanish in Brazil. Some people think Australians have English accents, but the accents are quite different; English varies greatly even in different parts of the United States.

That's why using a single audio file—which is the temptation presented by IT professionals—won't suffice for a company's diverse locations. The locals can tell the accent difference immediately, so we do our homework: We learn about a region's dialect and reach out to our contacts to find someone who can deliver the proper annunciation for our communication networks. We can access professional Hollywood casting shops for voice-over actors in order to achieve the correct image and brand for the company.

Our clients also can choose among voice-over actors with different styles according to the image they want to project, whether it's friendly, authoritative, sincere, perky, or a range of attributes. An on-hold network, after all, is about branding and image.

TruMusic

Branding and image also are why the style of music is important, too, whether it's music played overhead via in-store broadcasting or on an on-hold network. Because both are highly effective point-of-sale methods, it is essential to maintain control over the atmosphere. With our TruMusic service, we offer the flexibility to do it right.

A client should choose a music style consistent with the company culture. Back in the days when companies plugged the radio into their intercom systems, different employees would switch stations to suit themselves—and if you're trying to sell Cadillacs, the last thing you want to do is play Snoop Dogg to your customers. And, as we have discussed, there's another big reason not to do that: Even today, some restaurants and nightclubs that play the radio—and some on-hold providers, too—are finding themselves sued for copyright infringement. Don't make that mistake: You need access to a wide variety of licensed music styles.

Customers, after all, have a variety of tastes, so if you slap just any music onto your overhead or On-Hold Network, you could destroy that precious sales environment. That's why you often hear the disparaging comment, "Oh, that sounds like elevator music." It's about the most dismissive thing you could say about a song. At the root of that impression, once again, are those sound-system engineers who didn't understand the importance of marketing. You want to keep the music consistent with who you are as a company.

With TruMusic, we work closely with our clients to brand their concept. The service provides our clients with a dependable, licensed music stream from major labels, and they can custom-design the format. There's no equipment to purchase: The system doesn't use a CD player, and there's no satellite feed with its associated problems.

For your On-Hold Network, our website offers our clients a selection of many musical styles, but we advise against recognizable music. Here's why: Imagine yourself on hold, and you start to hear a melody, one you've heard so many times before. You tap your fingers. Or, if you hate the music, you might start drumming your fingers. Either way, it's not exactly drawing your attention back to the company, is it? You spend your time either humming along as you go back to whatever diversion you were involved in while waiting, or you set the phone aside to avoid having to be tormented—and you might not even hear when somebody does come back on the line. You have been further disengaged. The goal is to keep you constantly thinking about the company, and what the company is up to.

To use the music, we subscribe. We cover the music licensing fees monthly through ASCAP, BMI, and SESAC. We hire actual production houses. The music is in loops of thirty seconds to three minutes, and we pull them together. None of it is electronically created synthesizer sound: All the selections are done professionally by studio musicians.

In-Store Broadcasting

Phone On-Hold® offers more than music for in-store broadcasting. We provide professional scripting for the announcements about sales and other news that customers hear while shopping. Unless this is done with care and consideration, such announcements can become nothing more than background noise, repeated too often and in a grating style.

We call that interruptive marketing. I know how it feels when salespeople stop by my office without an appointment. They try to engage me but end up taking something important away from me: They're time bandits. That's how marketing like that feels, if you can call it marketing at all. It screams at you instead of enticing you. Instead, think of effective marketing as whispering into your lover's ear. You certainly don't want to scream, and you'd better say the right things or you'll mess up your chances. Likewise, you don't want to be interruptive to a shopper who has come through your doors or a prospect who has taken the time to call you. You know he or she is already considering your service or product. So choose your words carefully, as well as the type of music and type of voice.

We're here to help you do it right. Once we worked with a cell phone company that figured we'd done it wrong. To record its on-hold content, the company wanted to use a radio announcer and part-time comedian who was known for yelling out commercials. He used that same loud approach for the company's on-hold network, and customers were complaining. The owner was blaming us, but I explained that the content needed to be changed. The lesson, once again: Don't scream at people. Entice them and engage them instead. The music and words you choose, whether broadcast overhead in your store or used in your on-hold presentation, reflect the image of your company.

Aroma Scenting

One new wrinkle that we're considering for use in stores is called scenting. It can take the customer's shopping experience to an entirely new level. At a recent conference of the On Hold Messaging Association, Simon Faure-Field, a friend and colleague of mine from Singapore opened a briefcase with little vials containing a variety of scents. There are companies that manufacture them for use in places as diverse as grocery stores, hotels, and floral shops—and though one might think a floral shop's flowers would suffice, the idea is to entice patrons with that scent right away. Simon recently signed up cigar stores for the scent of leather: A discreet and hidden pump emits an occasional puff to enrich the atmosphere. Hawaiian floral scents are used in hotels there. Grocers can get a hint of oranges or peaches or broccoli.

Simon also had a vial with the smell of the ocean, and one called seaweed. He even had the smell of a sewage spill—I have no idea why—but most all were pleasant smells.

Here's how we might use scenting: We would offer to handle the entire customer experience for, let's say, a chain of grocery stores. We'd produce the on-hold network. We'd do the overhead music in the stores. And we would add scenting around the produce areas. In that way, we would coordinate the shoppers' experience and demonstrate how to enhance brand, image, and return on investment.

Voicecom

With our Voicecom service, we provide yet another effective way to focus on brand and image. This service provides our clients with telephone numbers for their voice mail, including toll-free numbers that they can call to check for any messages. Using a professional announcer, we create and record the productions in a manner designed to be attractive to the caller. We want our clients to sound and be different than their competitors.

Voicecom gives our clients flexibility with their messages while maintaining that professional poise. If you're going on vacation, for example, you just call us with the details and we will change the message, making sure it is presented well. Then, per your instructions, we resume the previous greeting after you have returned from your vacation.

A particularly useful feature of the Voicecom service is that it also works in concert with your e-mail service. When somebody leaves you a message, the system records it and sends the audio file to the e-mail of your choice so that you can click and listen to it there without having to dial in.

Conference Calls

We also offer conference-call capabilities to our clients, with a feature for recording those important virtual meetings. Here's how it works: You dial a toll-free number and enter the PIN that you are given to open the door to your specific conference "room." Your name is announced as you enter, and other participants from far and wide are introduced as they, too, come into the room. If you'd like a recording, that can be set up at the press of a button before you begin, and when the conference has concluded, you are sent a file that you can review at your leisure.

Telebroadcasting

Telebroadcasting is a service we offer that you might know as robocall, which stands for robotic call. It's the type of call you get during election season. Telemarketing has a bad name, and we use the service differently. We don't want to be interruptive. We only sell it to businesses, and we broadcast only to the base with which they have a relationship. We don't dial to residences. We don't dial to consumer houses. But a business that already has a relationship with a customer can legitimately call that customer to announce new products, for example, or a store opening or sale.

The hardware store, for example; focusing on contractors, gives us a list of businesses that they have worked with before to whom we send out a recording announcing a sale "we want to invite and inform you about an incredible sales event we have going on this weekend." It's informational, not a hard sell. After all, it is a non-sales environment. Thousands of calls at a time can go out. It's very effective if it's done right. It wouldn't work if the message were way too long and pushy. That could destroy the companies brand and image; however, done correctly it could clearly build brand awareness and customer loyalty. We want your customers to feel respected—and that's crucial if you expect to see them again. Through this service, they will appreciate the invitation to take a look at what you're offering. No need for a hard sell. Your relationship is what sells.

CHAPTER NINE

What To Look For In An On-Hold Provider

A ny out-of-work disc jockey, and there are plenty of them, can take music and do a voiceover to create an audio file, but if you are in the market for a quality on-hold network for your company, you want to find a provider who is doing more than just making sound to slap on your system. You want to hire someone who understands who you are—your brand, your image—and who is creative enough to project that well for you. You want someone with business savvy who appreciates all the hard work you've put into that image and who will help you preserve it. You want, in short, a bona fide provider.

You also want a company that has some staying power. Sometimes a customer will sign up for what seems to be a great deal and pay a few thousand dollars and then the provider just disappears. It was never legitimate. You can find one-person operations that outsource everything. Or you can find someone making recordings in his house with no real thought given to the creative process. And if that's what your value is, those people are out there.

OHMA membership indicates professional standards within the industry. We
call that the trademark of assurance.
It's like the Good Housekeeping Seal of
Approval.

Or you can look for companies such as ours, where we do have a building; we do have employees who show up every day; we do pay taxes; we do pay vacations; we do pay for medical benefits; and we have staying power. We have been around for over 25 years. If you are a business with a track record that does have a marketing department and does believe in maintaining your brand, you want to use a company that's similar to ours. Let the guy with a single location who doesn't care about his image hire that outsourcer.

The only indicator of professional standards that we have in the on-hold industry, outside of the clients whom we serve—is membership in the On-Hold Messaging Association. It is the trademark of assurance. If you are a member, you have exhibited acceptable business practices. It's like the Good Housekeeping seal of approval.

To gauge a provider's creativity, ask this:
"Do you have onsite studios and onsite
talent, or do you outsource it?"

But even if it is a member of the association, make sure the provider understands the concept of branding and not just "thanks for holding." The provider should be willing to tailor the message to precisely what the client needs.

The provider should be asking questions about your company and have a discovery process in place to dig deeply into what your business is about. Be concerned if you hear something like, "Well, just give me some information and we'll craft a script for you." What you want to hear is: "Let's take a look at your website, let's take a look at your printed material, let's look at some of the things you've already conventionally done in the marketplace." At Phone On-Hold®, we study that information to figure out what the company is saying about itself—and then we act accordingly. We conduct a Client Needs Analysis. Any on-hold provider that knows what it's doing will take an approach like that.

To gauge a provider's creativity, ask this: "Do you have onsite studios and onsite talent, or do you outsource it?" Outsourcing is big in business today. It technically can save money—for the company, not the consumer—but requires a much longer turnaround time. Companies like mine have studios in-house and talent in-house. A client can call at 9 a.m. and we can tailor the message to the request within fifteen minutes, whereas the task would take days if we out-sourced. I'm not saying outsourcing is bad, but clients have to decide if they care whether the provider gets to know them and tailors the service to reflect the company culture.

It's important as well to ask about the equipment that the provider uses—but again, our philosophy is that it's really not about the equipment; it's all in the fulfillment. A business misses the point if all it considers is the equipment. Of course, the type of equipment used does help to show the sophistication of the provider. Some are still e-mailing MP3 files and delivery systems in which the client has to get the audio content to play, whereas what we use is all remotely loaded and the end user doesn't have to do anything. The equipment should meet the latest standards—but remember: Even if it's the fanciest on the market, if you use it to annoy your callers, it avails you nothing.

It's important, as well, to ask about the equipment that the provider uses—but again, our philosophy is that it's really not about the equipment; it's about the content.

Also, consider how long the provider has been in the business. Some people decide they want to get in this business and they try it a few times but before long give it up, leaving their clients adrift and with a bad experience. Remember not all "On Hold Content Providers" are created equal. That's another advantage of looking for a provider who has membership in the On-Hold Messaging Association: To join, a provider has to have been in business for five years. Ask the provider about written strategic objectives and business models for their company. If they don't have one it may make you think twice before you engage them in business.

Among other ways to tell the difference between providers is this: Some will advertise "no monthly fees" or claim that "we'll keep your rate the same forever," or tell you that "for $325, you will own the equipment and can have the production." Those are generally smaller-minded companies that don't understand the value of an

On-Hold Network. You will be better off with companies that charge very little up front but do have a monthly fee: That's necessary to license music, continually service the account, and update the audio content. Such services are critical, and without them you are buying trouble and potentially tainting your company image.

Whenever you come across a sales pitch that is based on price instead of service, you are dealing with a much less sophisticated provider. When a prospect tells me, "Well, I can get something a lot cheaper from your competitor," I respond: "Sure. Absolutely you can. And if that's the value you want, if that's how you see your company, if that's what your image means to you and you're okay with that, then by all means go with the other guy."

Whenever you come across a sales pitch that is based on price instead of service, you are dealing with a much less sophisticated provider.

Let's suppose you run an auto-body shop, and you're highly regarded and proud of the quality of your work. A customer brings in a Mercedes, and you're going to charge $2,500 to fix his dented fender. "Why should I go with you?" he asks. "The shop down the street will do it for $1,000." You'd probably want to respond, "Go there, then, pal, because you're sure going to get your money's worth, which is a poor paint job."

At Phone On-Hold®, we sell to people who appreciate quality. I try to get prospects to understand that the audio content is the most important. You can get cheaper services—but just as that Mercedes owner has to consider how much value he places in his car, you need to decide how much value you place in your company. Sometimes I'll give prospects a list of other providers and concede that, sure, they can find lower fees. But if they value what their company does, and their company's image, then they should find a provider that likewise values what it does. With such a provider—and there are many good ones—it's a whole different experience.

Any legitimate on-hold communication business should have a long list of satisfied customers. There's a reason that the Hyatt uses a company like ours; there's a reason Costco Wholesale uses us; there's a reason that a Domino's Pizza franchise uses a company like ours. We fill a unique niche and provide a powerful and effective communication tool.

> **With so many companies trying to do more with less, they end up buying an On-Hold Network that they cannot operate. The project sits on somebody's desk.**

When you hire an on-hold provider, you should expect it to understand that thoroughly. You are hiring a servant who will advance your interests and save you time. And time, again, is a valuable asset for any business. It must be used wisely. With so many companies trying to do more with less, they end up buying an On-Hold Network that they cannot operate. The project sits on somebody's desk.

At Phone On-Hold® Marketing Systems and any other bona fide provider, we know how to get it done. We know how to capture the essence of your image and communicate it to your prospects and customers right at the time they are calling and thinking exclusively about you. Our goal is to give you that sophistication and yet make it easy for you so your staff is not burdened with yet one more thing to do.

Choose us, or choose one of our competitors, but choose well. Hire someone who understands how doing it right can enhance your image, brand and professional reputation.

IMAGINE a Better Way to CONNECT

T echnology is marvelous, and it can bring you the world, and it can take you to the world. But it's nothing without the human touch, without one person connecting to another and being sensitive to what other people need and want or don't need and want. That's the essence of effective marketing. And that philosophy goes way beyond business, into all aspects of life. Without the human touch, life is sterile.

Those smart folks who design the systems and put the wires together also tend to become decision makers in this industry. As we have seen, however, they don't think from the point of view of image and branding. They tend to be pragmatic, feeling that if callers have to wait, it doesn't much matter what they listen to. The mechanics and electronics of how the system operates are more important to them than what the caller experiences. They just want to make the thing work.

The engineers thought they saw ways to make money by com-puterizing and automating and taking the reception desk out of the equation. They came up with the auto attendant. They took people away. The human touch was lost. Today, the technicians and engineers are thinking the same way as they come up with ever more advanced software and systems. They are oriented toward machines, not people. That's why you get "press one for this, two for that, three to hear it again"—and four to lose your mind. The way it's done just irritates the caller.

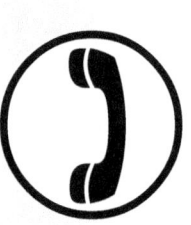

What people dislike isn't being on hold. They dislike being ignored and wasting their time. What's annoying are insincere apologies followed by claims that the company appreciates their business.

That's what has led to the perception that people just can't tolerate being on hold. But being on hold can be a cool experience. If a prospect proudly proclaims to me, "We don't put people on hold," I respond, "Too bad, because you're missing an opportunity."

What people dislike isn't being on hold. They dislike the unpro-fessional experience that most deliver to them when they are on hold. Everybody expects they'll have to wait sometimes. What's frustrating is when that wait feels like wasted time. What's annoying to them are insincere apologies followed by claims that the company appreciates their business.

All of that is so unnecessary: The time waiting on hold can be made quite enjoyable and informative. It's essential that a company make sure of that. After all, it has spent a lot of time, money and energy getting that phone to ring, so now's not the time to ignore or offend the customer. Nobody likes being put on hold because most businesses do not create the proper experience, but if that experience is handled properly, callers will gain a completely different perspective on the company that will pay dividends in loyalty and repeat business.

> **On-hold time can be made quite enjoyable and informative. It's essential that a company make sure of that.**

What you want to do is communicate with your callers. Let's say you're waiting on hold and you hear an interview with the president talking about how he got into business, his passion, and why his company is different. That's not a waste of time: That's educational and engages the caller. It builds loyalty and a relationship between the business and the consumer. And frankly that is what makes the world go around.

During that time, the caller might even get an answer to the question about which he called in the first place or learn that the information is readily available on the company website. That makes life easier for both the caller and the company. The caller gets useful information, and the staff can concentrate on service, which should be its focus, rather than on answering standard questions.

When my company comes in to help a client, we sometimes find the managers do have a good handle on branding and a workable On-Hold Network. They understand the marketing potential but want to make it even better. That's a particularly satisfying aspect of what we do: We look for the voids in service that we can help to fill so the company can truly capitalize on this opportunity. To me, it feels as if I'm working on a fine mahogany boat that has been taking in a little water through the planking: I fill those gaps and make it seaworthy.

Ensuring that our clients get a good connection with their callers is what we do. Yes, we make sure your system works smoothly. But beyond that, we make sure you connect with a human touch.

Ensuring that our clients get a good connection with their callers is what we do. Yes, we make sure your system works smoothly. But beyond that, we make sure you connect with a human touch. We create your on-hold network presentation so that the caller feels engaged and respected and appreciated. We eradicate any impression that you're turning your back on your callers at the very moment they're most interested in you.

If the presentation is done in an engaging way, the customer and the company build a better bond. As loyalty grows, so does the bottom line. A good on-hold network can bring you impressive improvements in customer relations, repeat business, and revenue.

At Phone On-Hold®, we know our clients have plenty of ways to spend money: supplies, equipment, labor, insurance, real estate. Spending money on your telecommunication system might not seem a priority, but remember: This is not a phone upgrade.

Rather, it's an advertising, marketing and communication program like no other. It distinguishes you from your competitors, giving you a whole different sound. It reaches people who, by definition, are interested in talking to you. It's a salesperson intimately familiar with your company and all it can offer, who makes the perfect pitch every time, and who never gets frustrated or tongue-tied. Why would you want to sound like everyone else?

A progressive on-hold network marketing system is an investment in your success. Remember it is really about you.

It's a salesperson intimately familiar with your company and all it can offer, who makes the perfect pitch every time, and who never gets frustrated or tongue-tied.

Recommended Reading:

The Telephone Doctor—Nancy Friedman

E-Myth Revisited—Michael Gerber

No Lie—Truth Is the Ultimate Sales Tool—Barry Maher

How can you use this book?

MOTIVATE

EDUCATE

THANK

INSPIRE

PROMOTE

CONNECT

Why have a custom version of *Holding Power*?

- Build personal bonds with customers, prospects, employees, donors, and key constituencies
- Develop a long-lasting reminder of your event, milestone, or celebration
- Provide a keepsake that inspires change in behavior and change in lives
- Deliver the ultimate "thank you" gift that remains on coffee tables and bookshelves
- Generate the "wow" factor

Books are thoughtful gifts that provide a genuine sentiment that other promotional items cannot express. They promote employee discussions and interaction, reinforce an event's meaning or location, and they make a lasting impression. Use your book to say "Thank You" and show people that you care.